'An entertaining guide by a real expert, with a lot of ideas for writers and film/TV to try' – *Promoting Crime Fiction*

'… a fabulous little book that is like a roadmap of Europe crime fiction' – *Crime Squad*

'Fascinated by Scandinavian crime dramas? Go to this handy little guide' – *News at Cinema Books*

CRITICAL ACCLAIM FOR *NORDIC NOIR*

'Entertaining and informative companion… written by the person who probably knows more than anyone alive about the subject' – *The Times*

'Highly accessible guide to this popular genre' – *Daily Express*

'The perfect gift for the Scandinavian crime fiction lover in your life' – *Crime Fiction Lover*

'A comprehensive work of reference' – *Euro But Not Trash*

'Readers wanting to get into Scandinavian crime fiction should start with Forshaw's pocket guide to the genre' – *Financial Times*

'Essential (book) not only for lovers of Scandinavian crime fiction but also for anyone who appreciates and wants to expand their knowledge of the genre' – *Shots Mag*

'If you feel drowned by the tsunami that is Nordic Noir but want to know who or what is the next big thing, get this book' – *Evening Standard*

CRITICAL ACCLAIM FOR *BRIT NOIR*

'Unsurprisingly Barry Forshaw's *Brit Noir* is a wonderful reference book that any self-respecting and serious connoisseur of crime fiction needs to have on their bookshelf' – *Shots Magazine*

'*Brit Noir* is a book to dip into but also, as I did, to read from cover to cover. I've always considered Forshaw to be an honest reviewer and the book very much reflects his personality. It made the book a stimulating and, at times, amusing read' – *Crime Pieces*

Also by Barry Forshaw

Nordic Noir
Euro Noir
Brit Noir
Italian Cinema

American Noir

The Pocket Essential Guide to
US Crime Fiction, Film & TV

BARRY FORSHAW

POCKET ESSENTIALS

First published in 2017 by Pocket Essentials,
an imprint of Oldcastle Books Ltd,
PO Box 394, Harpenden, Herts, AL5 1XJ
www.pocketessentials.com

A CIP catalogue record for this book is available from the British Library.

ISBN
978-1-84344-918-8 (print)
978-1-84344-919-5 (epub)
978-1-84344-920-1 (kindle)
978-1-84344-921-8 (pdf)

2 4 6 8 10 9 7 5 3 1

Typeset by Avocet Typeset, Somerton, Somerset TA11 6RT
in 9.25pt Univers Light with Myriad Pro display
Printed in Great Britain by Clays Ltd, St Ives plc

For more about Crime Fiction go to www.crimetime.co.uk / @crimetime.uk

Contents

Foreword: Showdowns on Main Street – James Sallis   9

1. Introduction   11

2. American Crime Writers   14

3. Selected Crime Films and TV of the New Millennium   155

4. Author Interviews   175

5. The Thirty Best Contemporary US Crime Novels   189

6. The Five Best Contemporary US TV Crime Shows   191

Foreword
Showdowns on Main Street

James Sallis

America is a nation founded at one and the same time on violence and high ideals. Both run in our blood. Is it any wonder we're forever off kilter? A strange tribe, this, wishing to be left alone and apart in one breath, tasking itself to repair the world around it in the next, Henry David Thoreau and Clint Eastwood riding double.

The American detective novel developed in synch with our nation's movement from a rural to urban society. By definition, it concerned itself with the dark corners, basements and back rooms of our national experience – those poor stitches and loose seams that held the thing together. What you saw was never what you got. American life wasn't about apple pies, proper behaviour in the Hamptons and drinks at the club; it was about the repudiated, the pushed-aside, about men and women and communities on the run, never knowing which would happen first, if the sky would fall on them or the ground give way beneath their feet.

Coming as I did from a dual background in poetry and realist fiction, crime stories first attracted me for the power of their imagery and their underpinning. Mythopoetic, my professors back at university would have said. Tapping the subconscious: buckets lowered into a well of archetypes hardwired in us all. These stories were about the things that scare us most, as individuals and as a society, and at the same time about all the things, material and non, we believe we most want. Soon I began to understand, as well, that they are our truest urban fiction, that these stories speak of our cities and our civilisation, address what we have made of them and of ourselves, as do no others.

The quantity of fine work being done today, as you'll see within, is extraordinary. So is the wealth of viewpoints, voice, ambition and sheer reach – such that *genre* seems profoundly lacking to describe so rich a body of work. All writing, be it literary fiction or epic poetry, is genre. Over the years, both as writer and as critic, I've come to think of crime fiction simply as a literary mode. A mode is a specific manner in which something is experienced or expressed, a particular set of notes comprising the scale from which melodies and harmonies derive. Which seems to me a more fruitful way of thinking about and approaching the grand array of crime fiction.

The arts do not progress, they develop by accrual: circling back, refitting old clothes, refurnishing rooms. But there is today in crime fiction some of the best writing being done anywhere, work that honours its past while reaching far beyond.

Finally, any body of work depends for its vitality and enrichment as much on its readers as upon its writers, and the ones taking point there, making all our lives richer, are the critics, editors, commentators and anthologists. As editor of *Crime Time* and as wearer of many hats, Barry Forshaw has introduced us to the best of current writing, helped us parse the roots and branches of the Nordic mystery, again and again has led us to broader understandings of films and novels.

When quite young I was oddly short and small for my age. My woodworking father, who'd given me the nickname Runt, built a pair of stilts so that I could be, in my mind and in my secret life, taller. What my dad did for me, our arts do for us all. They give form and vitality and validation to secret lives within us. Barry knows that. He has never, even for a single moment, lost sight of how important it is.

1: Introduction

The Big Country

The best crime novels can provide – as well as consummate entertainment – incisive and penetrating guides to the countries in which they are set. And nowhere is this syndrome more true than in American crime fiction, which freights in among the detection, betrayal and rising body count a detailed picture of US society. And it's a picture, moreover, that provides unforgiving psychological and societal insights into this big country, a world away from the more constrained parameters of the UK. And the impulse behind this painting on the largest of canvases? Very often anger at political corruption, beginning with the scorching *Red Harvest* and *The Glass Key* of Dashiell Hammett. But that progenitor of the genre is not to be found within these pages – *American Noir* attempts to tackle the contemporary scene. You will find such writers as James Ellroy and James Lee Burke, both of whom write novels powered by indignation (Burke's contempt for the George Bush regime practically leaps off the page, and Ellroy loathes political correctness). In the twenty-first century, there are signs that writers are beginning to examine their divided country's dark comedy of the Donald Trump era; it's surely only a matter of time before such sardonic crime writers as Carl Hiaasen tackle this. But American writers have always been good at skewering demagogues (think of – in the non-crime field – Sinclair Lewis's *Elmer Gantry*, Budd Schulberg's *A Face in the Crowd* or Robert Penn Warren's *All the King's Men*), just as the books of Scandinavian writers such as Jo Nesbo anatomised the rise of the far right in their own countries.

Issues

The genre has often tackled hot-button issues affecting society – often more keenly than in more avowedly 'serious' fiction. Readers are given an imaginative access to the various strata of US society – from the alienated underclasses to the upscale haunts of the rich – and a complex panoply emerges. Several writers have used the apparatus of the crime thriller to examine post-Vietnam America, social instability and modern fears of terrorism. Such writers as George Pelecanos have tackled issues of race in uncompromising fashion, and the problems facing modern women in the US are rigorously addressed in the work of writers such as Sara Paretsky, while the role of professional women is central to the novels of Patricia Cornwell. None of these writers, however, have forgotten the first imperative of crime fiction: keeping the reader transfixed with a powerful, page-turning narrative.

The formidable bestselling authors mentioned above are the merest tip of the crime fiction iceberg; the American crime-writing fraternity is exhilaratingly wide and provocative, with edgy new writers constantly emerging, not least in the currently popular domestic noir genre. Let's face it, a book such as *American Noir* can only ever be a snapshot of a given moment in crime fiction, but I've tried to cover as many writers as I can. I've also included some interviews I've conducted with writers including James Ellroy and Karin Slaughter.

Definitions

As with the other books in my 'Noir' series, the 'reader's guide' format I've used has entries ranging from expansive to capsule form. The remit of this study, though, has been as wide as possible: every conceivable genre that is subsumed under the heading of American crime fiction is here, from the novel of detection to the blockbuster thriller to the occasional story of espionage (although they are the exception). And, again, as with other books in the series, several of the authors included here stretch the definition of 'noir' to breaking point (and beyond). My aim once again was to include as many writers as I could (although there are virtually no historical crime novelists, whom I hope to cover in a later book). And the spectrum ranges from the truly dark noir region to its less unsettling polar opposite, in whose pages bloodshed is notably less copious. And although they receive a separate mention along with other crime fiction colleagues at the end of this book, I feel a keen need to give a preliminary tip of the hat to my confrères J Kingston Pierce and Craig Sisterson for their invaluable input and suggestions. Thanks, gents.

American Noir is principally designed to be used as a reference book to contemporary US crime fiction. And 'contemporary' here means 'living', at least at the time of writing – if the Grim Reaper has been a-roving since I began the book, that's beyond my control. So, don't look for Dashiell Hammett or even (more recently) the late James Crumley – it was damned difficult just fitting living writers into the allocated page count here (and my *Rough Guide to Crime Fiction* covers the hard-boiled and pulp era). And, as always with this series, the text is not designed to be read straight through from cover to cover – though that's up to the reader. You pays your money, you takes your choice.

Brit Noir had a layout based on the locations in which UK crime writers set their books, while *Nordic Noir* and *Euro Noir* were arranged by country; it seemed to me that the most useful order for *American Noir*, however, was a straightforward alphabetical one (to avoid, for instance, a humongous mass of author entries under 'California').

But now, it's time to take that Greyhound on Route 66…

2: American Crime Writers

JEFF ABBOTT's publishers prided themselves on how their strikingly designed new jackets helped sell his books (the strategy was even used as a blandishment to lure new authors to the imprint: 'Join us and we'll give you Jeff Abbott-type jackets!'). But finally, of course, it's the writing that counts. Abbott, in fact, is an exemplar of one of the several ways in which a writer of crime thrillers can guarantee one crucial imperative: the reader turns to the next chapter. James Patterson (discussed later) has a simple strategy: extremely short chapters that invariably end with a cliffhanging situation. Harlan Coben and Gillian Flynn (ditto) tease the readers with a series of perfectly timed revelations that keep us glued to the page. But Jeff Abbott, in such books as *Panic* and *Fear*, has a double-pronged tactic: establish a tense and unusual situation in the first chapter, then orchestrate the developments in hypnotic fast/slow segments. *Panic* used this alternating tempo to deliver the taut tale of a man struggling to find out the truth behind the disappearance of his father and the death of his mother, and the lean, polished storytelling surprised those who thought Abbott was a debut author. In fact, he had seven books under his belt; efficient enough, though they hardly hinted at the top-notch practitioner he'd become. If *Fear* wasn't quite in the same league as *Panic*, it was still pretty galvanic stuff. The protagonist, Miles Kendrick, starts the book at the end of his tether – and things get worse from then on. In an echo of *Fight Club*, Miles is being taunted by his best friend Andy, who is threatening him with humiliation and violence. But Miles has killed Andy – or so he believes. Andy isn't there, except as a taunting voice in his mind. Miles is in the witness protection programme, concealing his whereabouts from mob killers, even as he tries to deal with the guilt he feels at his friend's death. He has one ace in the hole: psychiatrist Allison Vance, trying to pull him back to some kind of mental equilibrium while sorting out the traumatic events of the night of his friend's death. But an explosion in her office kills Allison and destroys Miles' chance of regaining his sanity. He finds himself in a desperate cat-and-mouse game with FBI operative Dennis Groote, a man whose own madness takes a much more lethal form than that of Miles. The key to his survival lies in cracking the truth of just how his friend Andy died. If the levels of tension engendered here don't match those of Abbott's *Panic*, that's principally because the earlier book set the bar high for any follow-up. Forget direct comparisons, and you'll find that those tube or bus stops will fly by unnoticed.

One of the most astute of psychological crime novelists, the energetic **MEGAN ABBOTT** is responsible for such trenchant and commanding books as *Queenpin*, *The Song Is You*, *Die a Little*, *Bury Me Deep*, *The End of Everything*, *Dare Me* and *The Fever*, the latter selected as one of the 'Best Books of the Summer' by *The New York Times*. A native of Detroit, she received her PhD in English and American literature from New York University. She has taught at NYU, the State University of New York and the New School University. Apart from her nuanced and incisive novels (more interested in the complex psychology of her characters than many of her confrères, who sketch such things in), Abbott is also the author of an influential non-fiction book, *The Street Was Mine: White Masculinity in Hardboiled Fiction and Film Noir* – notably more sympathetic to her male subjects than much feminist writing in this area – and the editor of *A Hell of a Woman*, an anthology of female crime fiction. Talking to her at the inaugural 'Noirwich' crime fiction festival, I found her depth of genre knowledge was quickly apparent. She has been nominated for many awards, including three Edgars, the Hammett Prize, the *Los Angeles Times* Book Prize and the Folio Prize.

CHARLES ARDAI may also be award-winning mystery writer Richard Aleas. Or he might like us to think it's the other way round. Ardai's pithy writing has appeared in publications such as *Ellery Queen's Mystery Magazine* and *Alfred Hitchcock's Mystery Magazine* and has graced anthologies including *Best Mysteries of the Year*. His first novel, a quirky piece entitled *Little Girl Lost*, was published in 2004 and was nominated for both the Edgar Allan Poe Award from the Mystery Writers of America and a Shamus Award from the Private Eye Writers of America; his second, bearing the Blakean title *Songs of Innocence*, was selected as one of the best books of the year by *Publishers Weekly* and won a Shamus Award. Both books were written as 'Richard Aleas'.

Routinely hailed (along with such masters as Ross Macdonald) as one of the heirs apparent of Raymond Chandler, Robert B. Parker sustained a truly impressive level of invention over a long career, his death in 2010 seemingly bringing to an end the classic tradition of the tough and sardonic private eye. But Parker's gumshoe was revivified in the talented hands of **ACE ATKINS**, one of whose Spenser novels, titled *Robert B. Parker's Wonderland*, had all the hallmarks of the original creator, with the detective encountering a mysterious and seductive woman (par for the course), a terrifying Las Vegas criminal and a plot involving some suspect land development. If the truth be told, even the great Parker's invention was flagging a touch on some of his later books, but his new amanuensis/successor has conjured all the energy of his predecessor's best work. What's more, Atkins has added a quirky new perspective of his own. Reader response was along the lines of 'Welcome back, Spenser.'

PAUL AUSTER has long been a writer who inspires a keen following among those drawn into the dark world of his novels. Auster readers accept both ambitious, exuberant books presented on large canvases and pared-down, lean fables that demand total concentration. *Travels in the Scriptorium* lies firmly within the latter category of Auster's work, and while its rewards are many, it's a novel for those coming to the author as long-term aficionados rather than new converts. It begins with an ageing man sitting in a room, with no conception of how he arrived there or how long he will be there. The room is sparsely furnished, and suggests both a hospital and a prison. There is a manuscript on a desk – and the old man (who we learn is 'Mr Blank') starts to read it, only to find that it begins by describing his exact situation. Various familiar characters drift in and out of this enigmatic narrative – the protagonists of early Auster novels (a familiarity with the writer's other work is a definite help here) – and the narrative itself begins to assume a variety of shapes. Is this a detective story, a genre of which Auster has proved himself to be a master? Or is it an existential fable, a modern-day equivalent of the philosophical investigations of meaning that Jean-Paul Sartre and Albert Camus specialised in? The answers are not readily forthcoming, but diehard Auster fans will be well disposed towards the challenge of identifying precisely what his agenda is.

Oh no! Not another serial killer thriller! If this was your response to *Hour Game* by **DAVID BALDACCI**, you were not reckoning on the fact that this one was written by a man who would rather give up writing than too obviously repeat himself – or, for that matter, copy other writers. Yes, admittedly, a lot of the territory here has been traversed before, but this isn't Thomas Harris-lite – *Hour Game* bristles with innovations that obliterate any sense of overfamiliarity, even if the grisly opening chapters come perilously close to things we've read about before.

Baldacci is a member of an army whose numbers appear to grow daily: lawyers who have forsaken the legal profession for the blockbuster thriller. A lot of forests have been needlessly felled to produce some very mundane work in this field, but Baldacci is one who made the right career move. In such books as *Absolute Power* (filmed by Clint Eastwood, playing a burglar who witnesses a US president becoming involved in a murder) and *Saving Faith*, the author has made his mark as a writer of great narrative drive. *Split Second* introduced Baldacci's series characters: the tall, athletic Michelle Maxwell and the brilliant aesthete Sean King, both ex-Secret Service personnel who were obliged to leave their jobs under a cloud. The duo encountered some pretty nasty things in that first book, but *Hour Game* added new levels of gruesomeness. Maxwell and King, having inaugurated a partnership that will utilise their individual skills, look into the disappearance of some highly confidential papers owned by the well-placed Battle family. The decomposed body of a young woman is found, arranged in a bizarre position, and two teenagers are bloodily slaughtered while having sex in a car. It seems that a serial killer is at work – and King and Maxwell soon learn that the Battle family is (needless to say) in it up to their necks.

So what's new here? Baldacci has come up with something we haven't encountered before: a murderer who utilises the various modus operandi of famous serial killers, such as the highly intelligent psychopath Ted Bundy and several other real-life monsters. And it goes without saying that the horrific narrative is dispatched with maximum effectiveness by the author. But then the question was: what else could he do to reinvigorate the serial killer genre?

With the genre-bending *Wish You Well*, Baldacci built in new layers of understanding in the characterisation. The Cardinal family suffers a terrible car accident in which the children (12-year-old Lou and seven-year-old Oz) survive, but their father is killed and their mother left in a coma. Despite the destruction of their lives, the children are offered hope when their great-grandmother decides to take them to live with her on her farm in Virginia. Soon, they settle into a happy rural routine until natural gas is discovered on the mountain, and their bucolic peace is shattered by local opinion condemning Louisa Mae for refusing to sell. Soon, the Cardinal family is locked in a bitter courtroom battle in which their survival is at stake. As in his previous work, Baldacci is particularly good at the dynamics of conflict within a family as much as external threat, and without ever trying to manipulate the reader's emotions, he soon has us involved in a dramatic and affecting narrative that deals with issues of personal choice quite as cogently as with the large-scale emotions of the plot.

The gifted **LINWOOD BARCLAY** is generally regarded as a Canadian author, although he is in fact US-born (and hence included in this study), and he locates his books in the northern US states bordering Canada. Barclay's speciality is to take ordinary people and gradually dismantle everything in their lives that gives them meaning. It's an ironclad tactic that worked repeatedly for Alfred Hitchcock, who is cannily evoked by the publishers. In *A Tap on the Window*, Cal

Weaver picks up an injured female hitchhiker on a rainy night, one of his son's classmates. But when she asks to use a restroom, the nervous young woman who emerges no longer has the bloody hand injury that she had earlier – it is not the same girl. And when a woman is found savagely killed, Cal is in the frame. This is the reliable Barclay firing on all cylinders, and is a reminder that implacable storytelling skill remains the single most important component of any crime writer's curriculum vitae.

Fear the Worst? Isn't that what all good crime novels should make the reader feel for the beleaguered protagonist – vicariously, at least? In this book, Barclay proved once again to be adroit in the strategies of putting the reader through the wringer (via the problems of his central character), and it's a trick that Aristotle knew all about: catharsis. Certainly, that thoroughly purged feeling (in a strangely pleasant way) is precisely what Barclay's writing delivers, very much in the fashion of the author's earlier *No Time for Goodbye* – a considerable success in Britain. His hero, Tim Blake, wakes up to what he thinks will be an ordinary day. It will, in fact, be a prelude to a nightmare. His teenage daughter, Sydney, is staying with him while holding down a job for the summer at a nearby hotel. He is suffering the customary divorced parent's guilt, and is hoping for a bonding period with his daughter. He is not worried when she does not return from the hotel, assuming that she is spending time with friends. But then it becomes clear that she is not coming home at all – and, to his horror, he finds that nobody at the hotel where Sydney Blake was supposed to be working has heard of her. The nightmare has begun – and in a deftly modulated progression from unease to tension to terror, Barclay takes the reader towards Tim Blake's final engagement with some very sinister people. It's a journey in which Blake is obliged to reassess everything he thought he knew about his daughter (and, inter alia, himself).

There is a particular kind of popular writing, unpretentious and couched in functional prose, which has just one agenda: to stop you turning off the bedside lamp, however heavy your eyelids. Ira Levin was the exemplar in this field (with such books as *A Kiss Before Dying* and the expertly crafted *Rosemary's Baby*). Barclay has got within hailing distance of the Levin class, taking his own sweet time in building the levels of apprehension in *Fear the Worst*, and some readers may become a little impatient. But those on board for the author's slow-burn tactics find that considerable dividends are paid.

Before penning her inaugural standalone, the intriguing *The Perfect Ghost*, **LINDA BARNES** wrote 16 mystery novels, a dozen featuring her tall, red-headed private eye Carlotta Carlyle (a distinctive character), and four featuring actor/amateur detective Michael Spraggue (shades of the UK's Charles Paris, as penned by Simon Brett). Barnes has also written award-winning plays and short stories. In the 1980s, Barnes won the Anthony Award for best short story ('Lucky Penny') and the American Mystery Award for best private eye novel (*A Trouble of Fools*).

NEVADA BARR is the writer behind the popular Anna Pigeon series, which is set – unusually – in various US National Parks, where the author has worked. There have been 19 books in the series, which began in 1993; *Boar Island* appeared in 2016. Barr has also written standalones. She has won the Anthony Award, Agatha Award and Barry Award for various books in the Anna Pigeon series, and has multiple Anthony, Dilys and Macavity Award nominations. Barr was born in the small western town of Yerington in Nevada, grew up on a mountain airport in the Sierras, and has an interest in the environmental movement.

The storytelling in such 'Body Farm' novels as *Bones of Betrayal* by **JEFFERSON BASS** (aka Jon Jefferson and Dr Bill Blass) is of the punchy and emphatic variety, with a nicely judged acceleration of tension; this will come as no surprise, of course, to those who have read other novels by the accomplished Bass. Deadly radiation has been found on a body, and Dr Bill Brockton and his assistant have to deal with it – despite the grave danger it places them both in. Tense and atmospheric fare with good detail.

BRETT BATTLES was born in southern California. His first novel, *The Cleaner*, was nominated for the 2008 Barry Award for best thriller and the Shamus Award for best first novel. He followed this up with

The Deceived, which won the 2009 Barry Award for best thriller. Battles admits to a variety of influences, from Alistair MacLean, Robert Ludlum, Stephen King, Graham Greene and Haruki Murakami to the science fiction authors Isaac Asimov and Robert Heinlein. His own work is lean and efficient.

An elderly father and his son. An unburied body in a coffin. A fogbound airport… From *The Iliad* onwards, readers have always been in thrall to the sheer power of incident-packed narrative. And this is not a skill possessed only by the writers on the slopes of Mount Parnassus: James Patterson has it, as does JK Rowling. Even Jeffrey Archer had it in his early books. But there is another riskier strategy for keeping the reader turning the pages, one inaugurated by the French *nouveau roman* and given an audacious reworking by the American writer **GREG BAXTER** in *Munich Airport*: ditch plot and action, and look at how the characters' surroundings – the world – influence their behaviour. Little happens here; basically, the principal figures are trapped in the eponymous airport with no chance of getting a flight – but the steady accretion of detail slowly reveals to us the secrets of their lives in quiet but mesmeric fashion. Baxter brought off this singular trick in the earlier *The Apartment*, and while the later book will certainly not be to every taste, those prepared to open themselves to Baxter's unspectacular method will find plentiful rewards. The narrator is an American expat who has been living for years in London. A phone call from the police informs him that his sister Miriam has been found dead in her flat in Berlin. And the cause of his sister's death is incomprehensible: starvation. A fortnight later, the narrator's ageing, difficult father and a sympathetic female American consular official are marooned in a strange and alien world – Munich airport – waiting for bad weather to clear and allow them to take Miriam's coffin to the US. We follow their attempts to discover what led to Miriam's appalling death.

If the above sounds unpromising as a scenario for a novel, that is to ignore the sheer authority with which Baxter marshals his material. The three central characters are beautifully drawn, their personalities unveiled for us not in artificial, melodramatic fashion but by understated revelation. Both Miriam and her brother had left

America years before and were living (respectively) in Germany and London. They had grown apart from their father since the death of their mother, and via the novel's flashback structure we begin to learn what made them the people they became. Without a trace of sentimentality we realise that this is a novel about the importance of family and how the existential loneliness of each of the characters has impoverished their lives. Greg Baxter paints this as a modern malaise, and the airport – fogbound, surrealistic and unwelcoming – becomes a metaphor for the outwardly well-ordered but empty lives of the protagonists. And although the novel is a study of grief and familial dysfunction, the final effect is life-enhancing. Baxter sometimes channels Robert Frost's 'road not taken': there is a melancholy element present in *Munich Airport* suggesting that certain journeys might have changed the fate of the protagonists. But there is, at the last, a hopeful epiphany...

As **JOSH BAZELL** no doubt expected, his publishers tried to build a head of steam for his debut novel, *Beat the Reaper*, the actual quality of the book hardly an issue. Fortunately, the book turned out to be a critical success, even if sales were not quite commensurate. What marked *Beat the Reaper* out from the rest of an increasingly overcrowded field was its nicely honed prose – streaked through with a mordant wit (highlighted by a series of pithy, and highly entertaining, footnotes – an unusual element in the thriller genre). The plot? Peter Brown is a young Manhattan intern who is not all he seems to be. He has a past – and as any reader of crime novels knows, the past never stays buried for long. Peter has had an edgy run-in with a mugger and a more congenial elevator one-to-one with a female pharmaceutics rep. But his most significant encounter is to be with a new hospital patient, Nicholas LoBrutto, a man who knows the truth behind Peter's artificially contrived façade. The young intern is, in fact, in the witness protection programme, and he remains in the gunsights of some unpleasant New Jersey heavies. And things are about to get very hot for both Peter and LoBrutto. Lively and inventive fare.

Readers might have been forgiven for groaning at the notion of yet another feisty female forensic scientist, particularly as **ELIZABETH**

BECKA's (aka Lisa Black) publishers hopefully invoked an ace practitioner of that genre, Kathy Reichs. But just a few pages into Becka's *Trace Evidence* dispelled doubts: the author (herself a forensic scientist) has parlayed her medical know-how into something that functions strongly in its own right, familiar though the material is. Evelyn James, pathologist for the Cleveland Medical Examiner, is investigating the death of a young girl who has been pulled from the river. The victim is chained, with her feet embedded in concrete. Then a young woman from the upper echelons of society vanishes, and Evelyn finds herself drawn into a case that exposes multiple layers of corruption and deceit. All of this is handled with an assurance that belies the fact that this is a debut novel.

Best known in the UK for his Bond pastiches, **RAYMOND BENSON** is the author of the 'Black Stiletto' sequence, the first of which was *The Black Stiletto* in 2011. He was the first American writer to be commissioned by the James Bond literary copyright holders, between 1996 and 2002, to take over writing the 007 novels. He published six original 007 novels, three film novelisations, and three short stories. Based in the Chicago area, Benson is a member of International Thriller Writers and Mystery Writers of America. He served on the board of directors of the Ian Fleming Foundation for 16 years.

New York-born **ALEX BERENSON** joined *The New York Times* in 1999, covering everything from the drug industry to Hurricane Katrina; in 2003 and 2004, he served two stints as a correspondent in Iraq, an experience that inspired his debut novel, *The Faithful Spy*, which won an Edgar Award from the Mystery Writers of America. He has since written a lengthy sequence of novels featuring his CIA operative John Wells as well as a work of non-fiction, *The Number*.

Regarding **BILL BEVERLY**, I suppose I should declare an interest: I was one of the Crime Writers' Association judges who decided that the author was deserving of the 2016 Dagger award for the remarkable *Dodgers* – at a judging lunch at which that decision was arrived at very quickly, even before the first course. As I wrote in the

Financial Times, Beverly's road trip from hell has quickly acquired a cult following. Its hero, East, is 16 and a lookout at a Los Angeles drug house. He is dispatched to Wisconsin to murder a witness, and the nightmare journey that follows is written in an unadorned style that is both poetic and caustic.

Beverly was born and grew up in Kalamazoo, Michigan (yes, UK readers, there really is such a place). He studied literature and writing at Oberlin College, including time in London studying theatre and the Industrial Revolution. He then focused on fiction and pursued a PhD in American literature at the University of Florida. His research on criminal fugitives and the stories surrounding them became the book *On the Lam: Narratives of Flight in J Edgar Hoover's America*. Beverly now teaches American literature and writing at Trinity University in Washington DC. After *Dodgers*, UK crime readers are keen for more from this unusual writer.

Surely everything that can be tried *has* been tried in the field of crime fiction? Hasn't every possible genre been exploited down to the last bullet and falling body? Not quite, as **FRANK BILL**'s *Crimes in Southern Indiana* satisfyingly proved. What we are given here was described by its publisher as 'Hill-Billy Noir'. And if that particular designation doesn't appeal, you are doing yourself a disservice if you avoid the book; this really is something new and exciting in a field that – it appears – is still capable of renewing itself. The setting is the heart of America in the present, struggling to come to terms with the changes and innovations (not all of them welcome) that have come with the modern age. The world that Frank Bill presents for us is a bizarre combination of old and new: modern technology and hi-tech laboratories coexist with dungaree-clad gunrunners and ruthless bare-knuckle fighters. The dramatis personae whose paths cross dizzyingly in this fizzing book is a memorable one. Scoot McCutchen's life is thrown into chaos when his wife becomes terminally ill; Scoot ends up savagely killing her (along with her doctor) and tries to hide in his home town before he decides (it seems) to atone for his crimes. Or, in another story (this is a collection rather than a novel), a man moves from respectable dog breeding to providing canine candidates for brutal fights, before his destiny intertwines with a Salvadorian criminal and the backwoods drugs trade. And these, amazingly, are two of the least scabrous entries in the book. Perhaps the most striking characteristic of Frank Bill's magnum opus is the surprise that the reader feels when discovering that, however outrageous that tale we have just read, the author is able to top it with the next one. It's not a book (as they used to say) for the squeamish, but readers of gamey, pungent crime writing will be in seventh heaven.

CARA BLACK's long-running Aimée Leduc private eye series, set in Paris, has accrued a considerable following. Black has collected multiple nominations for the Anthony and Macavity Awards, a *Washington Post* Book World Book of the Year citation and the Médaille de la Ville de Paris. Black was born in Chicago but has lived in California's Bay Area since she was a child. Her Francophile instincts were kindled by the Prix Goncourt winner Romain Gary, but her work has a highly individual character, with few discernible influences.

The talented **JAMES CARLOS BLAKE**'s *The Rules of Wolfe* was long-listed for the UK's 2015 Crime Writers' Association's Goldsboro Gold Dagger. The book is a powerful chronicle of the violent Mexican drug trade, and *The House of Wolfe* is equally memorable. There are so many disparate elements crammed into Blake's remarkable novel that it is at times in danger of bursting at the seams. But just when the reader might think that the author has over-egged the pudding in this catalogue of kidnappings, torture, gunplay and death, he unerringly steers the helter-skelter narrative back on course. And there is a highly distinctive voice at work; admittedly, Elmore Leonard and Cormac McCarthy seem to be in the DNA here, but Blake is his own man. The rain is pouring down in Mexico City when the members of a wedding party are kidnapped at the mansion of the groom's family. Low-rent gangster El Galán has ambitions to join a major cartel, and sees the kidnapping as a PR stunt as much as a money-maker. But one of the captives belongs to a family of outlaws, so things are about to become chaotic and bloody. *The House of Wolfe* is pungent and exhilarating.

STEVEN BOCHCO has been silent as a novelist for a dozen years, but his unusual debut novel *Death by Hollywood* enjoyed some attention, as it was from the creator of *LA Law* and *NYPD Blue*. Checking out his neighbours in the Hollywood Hills using his upscale electronic telescope, Bobby sees a woman having sex with a personable Latin actor, Ramon. He gazes on in horror as the woman appears to batter her lover to death. Bobby resolves to use the attack as inspiration for his latest screenplay, and, rather than summon the police, he enters the scene of the crime in search of background material. However, he finds rather more than he had expected and, armed with this knowledge, he sets about insinuating his way into the lives of the principal players. Bochco brings to bear both his unerring ear for dialogue and gift for intricate plotting, along with a true insider's knowledge of the machinations of Hollywood.

He's not just a celebrity chef. New York-born **ANTHONY BOURDAIN** is also the quirkily accomplished author of the novels *Bone in the Throat* and *Gone Bamboo*. His edgy bestsellers *Kitchen Confidential* and *A Cook's Tour* are not for inclusion in this study, but neither is a million miles away from the crime idiom.

Frank about the self-lacerating drug use of his youth, Bourdain's expertise in the kitchen (Supper Club, One Fifth Avenue, Brasserie Les Halles) has proved to be matched with genuine crime-writing acumen, quite unlike that of his peers.

The fact that two bestsellers by **MARK BOWDEN** (*Black Hawk Down* and *Killing Pablo*) have been made into successful films has certainly raised his profile as a writer of thrillers. Unlike many other practitioners of the genre, the reader has no idea what to expect with each successive title: his speciality is to strike off in new directions with each book, which is the case with the fast-moving and persuasive *Finders Keepers*. As with Bowden's previous books, his background as a reporter at *The Philadelphia Inquirer* is pressed into service, so that all background detail has the plausibility of such writers as Frederick Forsyth. His protagonist in this piece is blue-collar: Joey Coyle is a dock worker eking out an existence in Philadelphia while looking after his sick mother and attempting to deal with his own crippling drug habit. Setting out for a drugs fix, he comes across two strange yellow containers in the street. To his amazement, he finds that the containers are stuffed with over a million dollars in unmarked notes. Coyle hides the containers before he is spotted, and learns that they are part of the loot from an attack on an armoured van. Then Coyle does a strange thing: he begins to share the money with almost everyone he knows, from the woman he loves to strangers chosen at random, and even local criminals. As the newspapers begin to zero in on the stolen money, Coyle lives in terrified suspense: will he end his days a rich man? Or will the police (or, for that matter, the mob) get him? As well as delivering the standard thriller mechanics, Bowden's book is an intriguing meditation on the nature of greed, and the reader is forced to examine just what he or she would do in the circumstances in which Joey Coyle finds himself.

Those who have encountered the rangy American writer **CJ BOX** ('Chuck' to his friends) on his visits to this country have been charmed by his amiable, good ol' boy country manner, finessed by an ever-present – in the UK, at least – cowboy hat, guaranteed to garner attention in the literary salons of London. And while it wouldn't be true to say that all of this is a sham (Box is the real thing – he lives in rural Cheyenne, Wyoming, and is a rancher, hunter and guide to the outback), there is actually more to him than these accoutrements might suggest. Apart from anything else, Box is extremely well read and echoes ex-president Obama in being a man familiar with William Faulkner.

Such vintage writers as John Buchan (*The Thirty-Nine Steps*) and Geoffrey Household (*Rogue Male*) may also be on Box's reading list, as *Back of Beyond* sported the same vibrant response to countryside and nature (in which tense chases take place) as his venerable British predecessors. In fact, it is this talent for marrying locale to accumulating tension that has perhaps created such a massive following for the author in his native USA. And Box began to accrue a growing number of UK enthusiasts as his publisher embarked on an ambitious programme of issuing the writer's considerable back catalogue.

Back of Beyond begins on a rainy day in the Montana mountains. Flame gutters in a burnt-out cabin. Inside, a charred corpse smoulders. Detective Cody Hoyt, a man with the customary baggage of personal problems (including alcoholism), is the investigating officer, and finds complications in the fact that the body is that of his AA sponsor, Hank Winters. The idea that Hank has died accidentally after a return to the bottle is discounted by Cody. Drinking has led to Cody himself being disgraced in the department – particularly when he wounds the county coroner after a stakeout goes wrong. Even though he is suspended, the dogged Cody is not about to let the murderer of his friend enjoy his liberty. The killer is on a horseback trek into the heart of Yellowstone National Park – and, to add an even greater frisson, Cody's alienated son is also on the trek.

The texture that comes from CJ Box's assertive storytelling skills and his channelling of the great writers of the past (accomplishments he is wont to play down) complements the sheer excitement of dark doings against a threatening landscape. And while our initial response to the economically characterised Cody Hoyt may be 'Yet another alcoholic detective?', readers soon find themselves disregarding the cliché, such is Box's ineluctable grip.

The remarkable life of the writer **JOAN BRADY** is surely a fit subject for an autobiography, but until she writes one, we'll have to be content with highly assured thrillers such as *Venom*. We had already been acquainted with Brady's impressive skills in the much-acclaimed *Bleedout*, which had such writers as Jeffery Deaver and Val McDermid queuing up to scatter praise; *Venom* built on (and consolidated) the success of its predecessor – not to mention the author's Whitbread Award-winning *Theory of War*. Brady's heroine, Helen Freyl, looks after her bee colony and is the custodian of a unique venom that she has had since childhood. After the death of the man with whom she had a relationship, she takes on a job with a major pharmaceutical organisation. Then people at the company begin to die – and Helen realises to her horror that her own life is on the line.

Joan Brady has had her own problems with the effects of poisoning (hence the mention of her remarkable life), and transmutes her anger into a novel that has a quite remarkable grip. Her protagonists (including her male lead, ex-con David Marion) are sympathetic, and the evils of giant corporations (a favourite theme of John le Carré) make for satisfying nemeses. Powerful fare.

This writer was once awoken at 3am by a ring on my bell. I knew what it was. Vans had been travelling by night transporting clandestine material. And that closely guarded material would be available – after midnight – only to those who had signed non-disclosure notices. The premise of the new **DAN BROWN** novel? No, it's actually how reviewers such as myself obtained our copies of *The Lost Symbol*, the follow-up to the mega-selling, all-conquering *The Da Vinci Code*. And as I began to read it in (literally) the cold light of dawn, I wondered whether it was likely to match the earlier book's remarkable success. Certainly, *The Lost Symbol* folded in all the elements that so transfixed readers in *The Da Vinci Code*: complex, mystifying plot, with the reader set quite as many challenges as the protagonist; breathless, helter-skelter pace – James Patterson's patented technique of keeping readers hooked by ending chapters with a tantalisingly unresolved situation is very much part of Dan Brown's armoury; controversially penny-plain, unvarnished prose that was as unappealing to many readers as it was irresistible to others. And, of course, the winning central character, resourceful symbologist Robert Langdon, was back, risking his life to crack a dangerous mystery involving the Freemasons, who replaced the controversial trappings of the Catholic Church and homicidal monks of the previous book. While Dan Brown will never win any prizes for literary elegance, his prose is always succinctly at the service of delivering a thoroughly involving thriller narrative in vividly evoked locales – here, Washington DC.

Robert Langdon flies to Washington after an urgent invitation to speak in the Capitol building. The invitation appears to have come from a friend with copper-bottomed Masonic connections, Peter Solomon. But Langdon has been tricked; Solomon has, in fact, been kidnapped, and (echoing the grisly opening of the previous book) a macabre mutilation plunges Langdon into a tortuous quest. His friend's severed hand lies in the Capitol, positioned to point to a George

Washington portrait – one that shows the father of his country as a pagan deity. The ruthless criminal nemesis here is another terrifying figure in Brown's gallery of grotesques: Mal'akh, a powerfully built eunuch with a body festooned with tattoos. Mal'akh is seeking a Masonic pyramid that possesses a formidable supernatural power, and a pulse-pounding hunt is afoot, with Langdon stalled rather than aided by the CIA. Caveats? Pointless here: Dan Brown, comfortably the world's most successful author, is utterly critic-proof. And there's no arguing with the fact that he has his finger on the pulse of the modern thriller reader, furnishing the mechanics of the blockbuster adventure with energy and invention. Despite some excoriating reviews, the book broke sales records on its first day.

What's the essence of a strong crime novel? Various elements are important, but the crucial gift any crime writer needs is that key storytelling skill. Many crime novels these days are, sadly, sorely lacking in this regard. **SANDRA BROWN** may not be particularly well known in the UK, but she's been honing her skills over the course of more than 60 books – and *The Crush* shows how that element is second nature to her. Her protagonist here is Dr Rennie Newton, who finds herself committed to jury duty. As in the film of *Twelve Angry Men*, however, she offers a dissenting vote in the case of a killer, and her not guilty decision has terrifying consequences, both for her and for others. Shortly afterwards, one of her medical colleagues is brutally murdered, and the police begin to focus their investigation on the increasingly worried Rennie. She realises that the threats to her liberty – and her safety – are beginning to mount, and she reluctantly decides to call on the services of a wry and disillusioned detective who has his own dark agenda. And as Sandra Brown's smoothly engineered narrative moves ever more swiftly to its climax, it's clear that the various plot strands are on a collision course. The prose here is always brisk and no-nonsense, but this lack of any finessing actually pays dividends in terms of momentum. So don't pick up *The Crush* for elegance – but if a gripping crime tale with a strongly drawn heroine is to your taste, this is for you.

EDNA BUCHANAN made her mark on Miami's police beat for nearly two decades, and reported over 5,000 violent deaths, 3,000 of them murders. She has said: 'Nobody loves a police reporter. I've been threatened with arrest, had rocks and bottles thrown at me, and received threatening letters, subpoenas, and obscene phone calls – some of them from my editors.' Her work as a crime writer has been much better received. The true crime book *The Corpse Had a Familiar Face* was succeeded by her series featuring Britt Montero, the members of the Cold Case Squad, and Michael Venturi, the latter first appearing in *Legally Dead*, all of these series drawing on her Miami experience.

The Daughter Also Rises. When James Lee's daughter **ALAFAIR BURKE** arrived on the scene as a crime novelist, there were dark mutterings of nepotism – mutterings that were stilled when readers became aware of the quality of the work on offer from Burke's offspring. Jesse Kellerman, scion of another famous crime-writing dynasty, required several novels to prove that he's not in print simply because he's the son of the writers Faye and Jonathan Kellerman. Stephen King's novelist son, who writes as Joe Hill, has established himself more speedily. But carrying the mantle of being the daughter of James Lee Burke – possibly the most acclaimed writer of crime fiction in America – Alafair Burke had the most challenging task of all, with a crushing load of expectation. Interestingly enough, she needed no period in which to find her feet; her Samantha Kincaid series achieved instant momentum, and she quickly marked out her own territory – very different (and less profound) than that of her father. Her own writing identity is off-kilter and idiomatic – and notably distinctive. *Dead Connection*, the first in Alafair's Ellie Hatcher series, is a striking effort, barrelling along with considerable speed. Two women are killed in New York, both having arranged dates via an online dating service. Their killer has left signs indicating a connection between the deaths of the two women, and Detective Ellie Hatcher is moved to the homicide task force to track down a murderer with a vicious agenda. Also mixed up in things is the grandiose detective Flann McIlroy, a policeman seduced by the lure of publicity (a notion reminiscent of James Ellroy's *L.A. Confidential*).

McIlroy perceives Ellie as a key element in catching a man who wants to bloodily decimate the lonely women of New York. It's unlikely – nay, impossible – that Alafair could ever match the achievement of her father, but, on her own terms, she is an accomplished writer.

Let's face it – life is short, and you'll never be able to read all the books you want to read. So why not just cut to the chase and read **JAMES LEE BURKE**? When it comes to literate, pungently characterised American crime writing, Burke has few peers – hence his lengthy entry in this study. When his novels featuring Cajun detective Dave Robicheaux first appeared, the sultry Louisiana settings were something new in crime fiction, and the writing had a forceful yet poetic quality that differentiated it from anything else around. Robicheaux, too, was something new: flawed, yes, and given to some moralising observations that at times sounded like the American Religious Right (surprising from an author who clearly regarded Reaganite USA as a very dark place to be), but Robicheaux is the most fully rounded protagonist in modern American crime fiction. That's not to say that all is rosy in the Burke garden: some novels in recent years have suggested that the author might be on autopilot, and his series featuring lawyer Billy Bob Holland, while diverting enough, seems more lightweight.

Born in Houston, Texas, on 5 December 1936, James Lee Burke grew up on the Texas–Louisiana Gulf Coast. He was educated at the University of Louisiana Lafayette, and subsequently at the University of Missouri. Before writing for a living, he had a chequered career: oil refinery worker, journalist, social worker, among other jobs. Burke has also taught creative writing courses at Wichita State University. The author, who has struggled with alcohol problems (reflected in his protagonist Dave Robicheaux), has homes in both Montana and Louisiana; his daughter, Alafair (see above), has overcome accusations of riding on her father's coat tails and has made a mark in her own right as a crime novelist.

Like many a crime writer, James Lee Burke originally saw himself as a literary novelist – before he realised that he could address serious concerns (and finesse the quality of his writing) within the constraints of genre fiction. As with so many American writers, the shadow of William Faulkner fell across his work. In the 1960s and early 1970s, *Half of Paradise*, *To the Bright and Shining Sun* and *Lay Down My Sword and Shield* were laced with the brand of Southern Gothic that was Faulkner's speciality, and the critical response to the books was muted. Ironically, after Burke's subsequent celebrity as a crime writer, these early books acquired a considerable cachet, and first editions are now keenly sought after.

The first Dave Robicheaux novel, *The Neon Rain*, instantly established the credentials of the series, in terms of both its uncompromising intensity and its refusal to sit easily in any proscribed category. Robicheaux, attempting to come to terms with life back in the States after the horrors of Vietnam, had found solace in alcoholism but has managed to claw his way back to sobriety. He has had a lengthy stint working for the New Orleans Police Department, and has made more enemies than friends within the force. His day-to-day dealings with the lowlifes of the city have also left their mark, but (rather like Raymond Chandler's Philip Marlowe) he has been able to retain a core of untouched humanity that helps him survive the grim business of life. Over the course of the book, he becomes involved in labyrinthine plots involving arms dealing and drug scams, but his most difficult problem is dealing with a bent cop – his partner. Burke deals with issues of loyalty and betrayal with a forcefulness that James Ellroy brought to similar areas in *The Black Dahlia*.

The second Robicheaux outing, *Heaven's Prisoners*, offered little respite for Burke's beleaguered protagonist. Dave is now married, and he and his wife have a daughter – but things are complicated by the fact that his adopted daughter is an illegal immigrant. Then Dave's wife is savagely killed. The grim parameters drawn up in these early books leave Robicheaux with the legacy of guilt and pain that are the constants of his life thereafter. Despite the theme of redemption (often of a religious nature) that runs through all of the author's work, the overriding presence is that of evil – and it is Dave Robicheaux's job to extirpate this evil, even though it returns, in some form or other, with each new book.

Burning Angel centres on a mysterious notebook and stirs Central American guerrillas into the mix, while in *Cadillac Jukebox* Dave is offered a lucrative job by a political candidate – not, it has to be said, a career move that appeals to a man whose job is dragging secrets into the cold light of day. *Jolie Blon's Bounce* has Dave on the trail of a rapist and murderer, who may or may not be a small-time hustler; this is vintage James Lee Burke, though possibly a novel that recycles familiar tropes from the author.

Purple Cane Road is a novel that reminds readers that Burke is as much a literary stylist as he is a purveyor of flinty crime narratives. Here is writing of a rare distinction, filtering the tough concepts of Raymond Chandler and Dashiell Hammett (along with other unsung pulp heroes) through the ambitious literary prism of such American titans as Fitzgerald and Faulkner. Burke's writing is always shot through with psychological complexity; readers might become a touch blasé, so commonplace is that element today, but this book was a salutary reminder of the possibilities in what is loosely called the crime genre.

Robicheaux is here plunged into his most painful and personal odyssey yet. He learns that his mother Mae was a prostitute who was drowned in a mud puddle by crooked cops in the pay of the Mob. As Dave and his tough partner Clete Purcell investigate, they encounter State Governor Belmont Pugh, a fundamentalist preacher who regards politics just as he did his first job, as a door-to-door salesman; the terrifying Remeta, a super-intelligent hitman; and, most significantly, Jim Gable, owner of the mansion in the eponymous Purple Cane Road, who knows more about Dave's wife than Dave himself. As Robicheaux struggles through a morass of intrigue and double-dealing, he finds that coming to terms with his own troubled past becomes as important as identifying the killers of his mother.

Burke's strategy, as in such books as *The Neon Rain* and *Cimarron Rose*, is to subtly subvert the standard detective narrative, creating a seamy panoply of the darker side of American society. Alongside the customary imperatives of bloody violence and dangerous sexuality (not least in the uncomfortable circumstances of Dave's mother's squalid murder), Burke is able to address such issues as the growing chasm between black and white and the inequalities that have riven American society. Most of all, though, he is a storyteller of prodigious ability. If you're tempted to groan at yet another recovering alcoholic protagonist, at least Burke does it better than anyone else (drawing on painful personal experience), and the use of language remains nonpareil.

By the time of *Pegasus Descending*, Dave's struggles with alcohol are a thing of the past, but he's still racked with guilt over a set of circumstances relating to his drunkenness. An old drinking friend, Dallas Klein, had become addicted to gambling and was forced to take part in an armed robbery. Klein died in the bungled heist, and Dave is convinced that he could have saved him. He finds himself once again in contact with those involved in this violent incident from the past, including Trish, Dallas's daughter, who has gone off the rails since her father's death; and the suicide of a girl to whom Dallas owed money soon has Dave up against two influential criminals. All this is handled with the panache that we expect, and, as usual, myriad elements are mixed into this peculiarly heady brew. Burke has always been given to plots of such labyrinthine complexity that they make Raymond Chandler read like Enid Blyton, and *Pegasus Descending* is no different. The two powerful heavies who Dave encounters have a perfectly bourgeois desire to shield their sons from the destructive elements in their own lives, and when the boys become involved with a black drug dealer (drawn in a nicely equivocal fashion), bloodshed is inevitable.

New readers may find the density of incident a little intimidating, but those already in thrall to Burke's spell will feel that they are getting their money's worth. We get the razor-sharp social observation that is one of the incidental pleasures of Burke's writing, and an extra bonus comes in the threatening presence of a natural calamity that is threaded through the book: Hurricane Katrina – although it is treated more as an atmospheric disturbance than the political metaphor it might once have been for the author (George Bush gets off a touch more lightly here than Ronald Reagan did in previous Burke novels).

Burke's Robicheaux books are his signature work, but he has featured other protagonists, such as Texas lawyer Billy Bob Holland in the impressive *Cimarron Rose*. Holland is an attorney in the Texas town of Deaf Smith. An ex-cop, whose career ended under a cloud, he becomes involved when his wayward son appears to be railroaded for the rape and murder of a young girl. *Heartwood* focuses on a rodeo cowboy whose life and career have gone adrift – and Holland has to defend him when he is falsely accused of theft. Like its predecessor, this is a more intimate book than the Robicheaux novels, with a more quirky humour running through the narrative. In *Bitterroot* and *In the Moon of Red Ponies*, Burke utilises, respectively, malignant white supremacists and bigoted US senators as signal images of evil – the notion of evil is ever present in the author's work, and not just as an abstract concept.

White Doves at Morning is one of Burke's most poetic non-series (and non-crime) books, built around his own ancestors, privileged slave owners. The black slave at the heart of the narrative, Flower Jamison, is one of the author's most fully rounded creations.

Finally, though, a footnote. As a counterweight to the encomiums above, it should be pointed out that many readers – even Burke admirers – find the religious undertones of his work intrusive. Unlike the similarly Catholic Graham Greene (who never makes his characters' crises of faith or doubt tendentious or an advertisement for the Catholic faith – quite the reverse, in fact), Burke could be accused of interleaving his narratives with a slightly religiose quality – a sort of veiled, hopeful exemplar for a more Christian life that the secular reader may find difficult to accept. But – as with Greene – non-believers need not hesitate. Great writing rises above its ideological underpinnings – and that's very much the case with James Lee Burke.

The critically acclaimed **JAN BURKE** has tried her hand at a variety of genres: crime fiction, supernatural thrillers, short stories. She bagged one of crime fiction's top baubles, the Edgar Award for best novel, for *Bones*. The author was born in Texas but has lived in southern California in coastal cities, a variety of which were combined to create her locale Las Piernas, stamping ground of her protagonist, hard-working journo Irene Kelly.

In *The Night Season* by **CHELSEA CAIN**, the banks of the Willamette River have burst and the city is on high flood alert. Already people are dying in the ever-rising floodwaters, but there is a victim who was not killed by the water – she died before her body took the plunge. As other bodies begin to appear, police detective Archie Sheridan becomes aware that Portland may be dealing with a vicious serial killer. Also on the case is reporter Susan Ward, whose leads are taking her into very dangerous territory. This is unique, off-kilter fare from a gifted young American writer – who has been known to dress in the hippie apparel of her parents.

When the success of *The Sopranos* fuelled our fascination with all things Mafia-related, it was hardly surprising that there were plenty of novels appearing designed to slake our interest. **LORENZO CARCATERRA** is one of the most reliable practitioners of the gangster genre, and such books as *Gangster* and *Street Boys* have demonstrated his remarkable talent: pithy, idiomatic dialogue, razor-sharp plotting and vividly drawn characters. *Paradise City* delivered all those elements in what may be his most distinctive book. Neapolitans have granted New York the soubriquet Paradise City, but for a tough Italian policeman, Carcaterra's protagonist, arriving in NY, it's hardly that. As Lo Manto tracks down a missing niece, he finds himself in the throes of an ancient Mafia feud that devolves on his own history. With its cross-continent locales (from Italy to Manhattan) handled with equal panache, and a strongly characterised, conflicted central figure, *Paradise City* is pungent and powerful writing.

With *A Land More Kind Than Home*, **WILEY CASH**, who is a native of western North Carolina, produced a debut of raw and uncompromising heft, written in a totally persuasive argot. The follow-up, *This Dark Road to Mercy*, is every bit as accomplished and sports the same felicitous use of locale, conjured once again with some skill, with, at its centre, a totally gripping crime narrative.

With a respectable corpus of work behind her, **LINDA CASTILLO** has shown that she has literary staying power, with *Sworn to Silence* a key book. The setting is a placid Ohio town, Painters Mill, in which opposing groups of residents manage to co-exist: the religious sect the Amish, and the ordinary residents of the town, known (in distancing fashion) as 'the English'. But this is a Linda Castillo novel, and it will come as no surprise to the reader to realise that this peaceful town harbours dark secrets: over ten years ago, a sequence of savage killings tore the community apart and had a corollary effect. Young Katie Burkholder was a member of the Amish community but became aware that she could not live by its rules and strictures, and that her view of the world was not that of her coreligionists. Some 15 years have passed, and Kate has now become chief of police. This element of Castillo's novel already marks it out as different; the concept of the female Amish-turned-copper is a truly novel one and puts paid to any uncharitable thoughts that Castillo may have borrowed some ideas from the Harrison Ford film *Witness*, in which a detective solves a murder in an Amish community. In *Sworn to Silence*, the body of a young woman is discovered in a snow-covered field, and it bears a grisly mutilation: numbers have been carved into the stomach of the dead girl. She is the first in a line of victims, and the long maintained peace of the town is soon a distant memory. Kate Burkholder is a well-realised protagonist in an unusual novel.

If ever a writer deserved the epithet 'cult', it's **JEROME CHARYN**. With a relatively small body of work, Charyn has constantly striven to write books that are far more than just crime novels. His bleak and penetrating vision of human nature reads like a bizarre synthesis of Dostoyevsky and Dashiell Hammett, and his novels even present a fully worked-out world view – one, however, that offers little comfort. The Isaac Quartet is, in many ways, his magnum opus, and *Blue Eyes* has been acclaimed by such writers as James Ellroy as one of the most significant of crime novels. While always readable, *Blue Eyes* never strives to be commercial and is full of penetrating detail, with the characters' motives (however murky) always totally believable. The theme is trust and betrayal, but Charyn has much more to offer than the mechanics of the workaday crime thriller. The eponymous 'Blue Eyes' Coen is a police detective working out of the Bronx precinct that was his stamping ground. Child brides have been abducted, and the latest missing girl is the daughter of a very rich man. The evidence points to friends of Coen's, the Guzmanns, and his colleague, First Deputy Isaac Sidel, knows that only one man can sort out this baffling mystery. Betrayal, of course, is on the agenda, and in this stringently existential novel (with its pronounced Jewish ethnicity) the twists and turns come thick and fast. Inventive and perceptive writing pays off again and again in valuable overtones and implications. There are degrees of merit in the commercial novel, and Charyn can lay claim to some of the best writing the genre has to offer.

LINCOLN CHILD has made a mark with such books as *Death Match* and *Utopia*, as well as co-writing, with Douglas Preston, several straightforward blockbusters (including *The Book of the Dead*, *Dance of Death*, *The Cabinet of Curiosities*, *Still Life With Crows* and *Relic*). In the duo's *Cold Vengeance*, the protagonist is traumatised by the murder of his wife and is focused on retribution. His obsession takes him from the moors of Scotland to the bayous of Louisiana, and the search leads to disturbing discoveries about his wife – and growing levels of conspiracy that suggest that his own existence has been built on falsehoods. The pace of this entry in the series is more steady than usual, but the authors' willingness to take their time ultimately pays dividends.

The veteran American writer **MARY HIGGINS CLARK** has long enjoyed a reputation as one of the most accomplished and reliable of storytellers, and has gleaned a faithful legion of admirers for her impeccable plotting. Her younger colleague Alafair Burke (discussed above) is a very different kind of writer, overcoming a heavy burden of expectation (being the offspring of a celebrated writing parent) by strongly registering her own writing identity: quirky, personal – and very different from her heavyweight father, James Lee Burke. The two women are not, one might have thought, natural collaborators, but in the event they make a splendid team, and *All Dressed in White* is a real winner. Five years prior to the start of the narrative, Amanda Pierce was full of keen anticipation for her marriage to her college sweetheart Geoffrey. Amanda was on the point of inheriting her father's profitable garment company but then she suddenly disappeared. In present-day New York, Laurie Moran is searching for cases for her television series *Under Suspicion* and is well aware that a missing bride case will make for good viewing figures. She decides (unwisely, it transpires) to recreate the circumstances of the night of Amanda's disappearance, and suddenly the secrets of the past become very pressing – and very dangerous – for a variety of individuals. One thing that *All Dressed in White* does triumphantly is to come up with some fresh ideas for the over-taxed crime genre – and given that every theme has been explored so thoroughly over the years, that is no mean achievement. Both women's strong personalities are stamped on the narrative here, which delivers on many levels and prompts a wish for a continuation of this collaboration.

HARLAN COBEN's novels may be tough, but there's always a yearning for the comforts of relationships (particularly those in families) and that very human element is the perfect balance for the hard-boiled narratives that are Coben's stock-in-trade. His protagonist, detective Myron Bolitar, is one of the most fully rounded figures in modern crime fiction. Like the earlier *Tell No One*, *Gone For Good* starts with the return of a character long believed to have been lost, and we are again plunged into the mean streets of New Jersey with its colourful cast of murderers, gangsters and other unsavoury characters. Another recurring theme is the deeply ingrained suspicion of the mechanics of federal law enforcement, and Coben's protagonists finally have to rely on their own resources to survive. The plot has all the incidental felicities that we turn to Coben for, and (as usual) the requisite number of diverting twists to keep the reader off-balance. But most of all, it's the humanity of Coben's writing that distinguishes him from his crime-writing peers, and that's as important an element here as anything else. So many thriller writers concentrate on action and movement at the expense of all else, with the result that we don't give a damn about the characters or what happens to them. Coben's more character-centred approach is the polar opposite of such carelessness, and *Gone for Good* is as impressive as anything by the author.

Similarly, *Live Wire* demonstrates Coben's authority. As footballers and other super-rich types wield injunctions to keep their secrets buried, they may feel they are fighting a losing battle in a world of scattershot electronic dissemination. Perhaps they should try murder – it's a solution usually practised in crime fiction and seems to attain the desired effect – for a time at least. But, inevitably, the chickens come home to roost. Malicious Facebook exposures are at the heart of *Live Wire*. Coben, as is his wont, combines storytelling nous in the most venerable tradition with an *au courant* engagement with the modern world.

Myron Bolitar, once Coben's habitual protagonist, had been sidelined of late but was back in this book. Myron's juggling of multiple careers (sports agent and private investigator being his two main callings) has become ever more complicated over the years, and his reckless readiness to sacrifice equilibrium in his own private life to help friends and clients has come at a heavy cost. An anonymous Facebook posting makes scurrilous claims about the paternity of an unborn child – that of ex-tennis star Suzze T and her wayward rock legend husband Lex. The latter, unsurprisingly, jumps ship, and the heavily pregnant – and desperate – Suzze visits Myron, pleading with him to save her marriage. But as so often with Bolitar, his own jumbled private life has a way of interposing itself on his cases. He encounters his sister-in-law Kitty (married to a brother to whom Myron no longer speaks) and her son Micky. The latter is burning with anger at Myron, whom he regards as responsible for his parents' problems, further complicating an already incendiary situation. A dual search – and the issue of how lies can deform our lives – takes *Live Wire* into some very unsettling territory, in which Coben's hero even finds himself questioning his own identity.

Although the mechanics of the plot are handled with the customary aplomb, for most readers the real interest of the book will be Coben's readiness to turn around everything we thought we knew about his long-serving central character. And, frankly, this strategy is far more engaging than the putative main plot – something, no doubt, that Coben was fully aware of. His standalone thrillers have been enthusiastically received in the UK, as, commandingly written though the Bolitar books are, British readers often find it hard to relate to the world of American sports that is so central to them – not a problem, one imagines, for American Coben fans. But no such caveats are necessary here. The unsparing examination of Myron's identity in *Live Wire* shows Coben comfortably (to use a sporting metaphor) at the top of his game.

Finally, let's look at the standalone novel *The Innocent*, sporting some typically scabrous and witty dialogue – not to mention a characteristically teeming cast of characters. And, boy, is it a vintage batch here! Matt Hunter has been receiving compromising pictures of his wife from an unknown source, and he begins to realise that the woman he thought he knew is a stranger to him. At the same time, homicide investigator Loren Muse is called in to investigate the death of a nun, and finds herself in the uncomfortable position of having to deal with the Mother Superior who made her life miserable as a young girl. But some very strange elements are woven into this case – such as the fact that the nun had breast implants. Behind all this bizarre mystery are some very sinister figures, and something bad that happened in Nevada a decade before. Both Matt and Loren quickly find the stakes in this game are of the very highest. If your taste is for crime novels that can be relied upon to wrong-foot you in the most delightful way, you should pick up a copy of *The Innocent*. Or pretty well anything by Harlan Coben.

STUART ARCHER COHEN made his living as a private investigator for 15 years, and has a similar breadth of experience in the legal arena; the wealth of knowledge acquired paid off in the author's first novel, *The Stone Angels* (also published as *17 Stone Angels*), a tour de force of narrative precision and psychological acuity that burnishes the thriller genre afresh. Commissario Miguel Fortunato is dealing with both the death of his wife and the pending threat of retirement, looking back wryly over his turbulent years with the Buenos Aires PD. Fortunato has been involved – unwillingly – in the kidnapping of a foreigner, an action that ended badly. Subsequently, Athena Fowler, a resourceful American investigator, arrives in Argentina and it becomes Fortunato's job to help her look into the death of a novelist – an event that ties into his own dark past. And a colourful cast of very disparate characters is thrown in their way on what becomes a bloody quest. This is splendid stuff, with complex and conflicted characters dealing with various crises of conscience. And Cohen's refusal to deal in clichés is equally to be applauded – yes, we've had the odd couple duo of investigators before (many, many times – and it's one of the modern cinema's most warmed-over themes). But Stuart Cohen seeks and finds new wrinkles in the idea, not least because his adroit plotting papers over any over-familiar tropes.

MAX ALLAN COLLINS may have inaugurated his writing career with facsimiles of the work of the pulp writers he admired, but he has long emerged from the shadow of such influences and now produces truly individual and surprising novels – which is very much the case with *Seduction of the Innocent*, which functions as both a classic period hard-boiled tale and a clever commentary on the real-life hysteria that put paid to the American crime and horror comics of the 1950s. The title, of course, is a reference to the infamous anti-comics tome by Fredric Wertham, a publicity-seeking pundit of the era who formulated some extremely specious reasons to blame all of America's juvenile delinquency on such things as the EC Comics classic Crime SuspenStories. What Collins has done here is to create an ingenious roman à clef in which the key figures of that era feature in a murder mystery involving Jack Starr, a comics syndicate troubleshooter of the day. Along with Collins' lively text, there are some clever illustrations by Terry Beatty that unerringly capture the style of the EC comics that caused all the fuss in the middle of the last century, particularly one of EC's star artists, Johnny Craig. The whole thing is great fun, whether or not you are an aficionado of the comics of that era.

The sales of **MICHAEL CONNELLY**'s *The Lincoln Lawyer* shot through the roof after a UK TV book club selection. Existing Connelly fans (people of taste!), though, felt a tad superior to readers who discovered Connelly via this book – they were already familiar with the author's tough detective Harry Bosch who had appeared in a dynamic series of novels, though not in *The Lincoln Lawyer*. That book showcased low-rent lawyer Mickey Haller, and he's back in the equally accomplished sequel *The Brass Verdict*. But Connelly has something else up his sleeve this time – added value is in store for the reader when he springs a surprise on us. Mickey is smarting after the rigours of his previous case. Then fellow lawyer Jerry Vincent is murdered, and Mickey becomes the recipient of a highly unusual bequest: he has inherited all his dead colleague's clients. One of these is Hollywood mogul Walter Elliot, arraigned for the murder of his wife and her lover. Mickey is well aware that if he can pull this case off, the ensuing media hoopla will catapult him back to the front rank of his profession. Things, though, are not straightforward – and when the taciturn detective on the case suggests that the murdered lawyer was killed by one of his own clients, Mickey realises that his inheritance of this client list could be just as deadly to him as it was to Vincent. All of this is handled with the storytelling panache that has made Connelly such a reader favourite, but he's not taking any chances that we might think this second outing for Mickey Haller is less engrossing than *The Lincoln Lawyer*. So who is the hard-nosed detective on the case, obliged to work with Mickey? None other than Harry Bosch, protagonist of earlier Connelly classics. The interplay between the two men is as sparky as one could wish, though the author does lay himself open to one charge: that the two men are a little too similar. But it's a reservation that will not trouble the legion of Connelly fans. So who does he feature in his next book – Haller or Bosch? Who cares, if the writing is as energetic as it is here?

The earlier *Echo Park*, the twelfth book featuring the wonderful Harry Bosch, is every bit as entertaining; it's the realisation of Harry's troubled character that makes Connelly's books so memorable. Even the overfamiliar motif of an alcoholic detective is handled with skill, banishing thoughts of cliché. Back in 1993, a young woman vanished after leaving a Hollywood supermarket, and the case wound up with homicide detective Bosch. Thirteen years pass, and Harry is now in the Open/Unsolved Unit – although he's never forgotten Marie Gesto's disappearance. Harry receives a call from the DA's office: a man accused of two brutal murders is proposing a deal to avoid the death chamber. He will confess to killing a slew of other victims, one of whom is Marie. And Harry now finds that he must become close to a man he has both hunted and despised for years. This is Connelly doing what he does best: delivering a beautifully structured, richly atmospheric crime novel.

Why is it that as readers we are almost always intrigued by a novel that takes the form of a quest? Is it because literary quests usually have a satisfying resolution, unlike those in real life? One of the most compelling examples in some considerable time is launched in this completely seductive novel by **THOMAS H COOK**. Cook is one of those writers cherished by the cognoscenti, but whose name for many readers will suggest a travel company (hence, no doubt, the redundant 'H'). *The Quest for Anna Klein* raised his profile – though, one might argue, insufficiently, given his achievement. The search begins with Thomas Danforth, a man whose life appears to have been carefully laid out for him: successful importing company in New York in the 1930s; financial success; secure future. But then a friend from the government comes to him with a highly unusual request. Danforth is to facilitate the training of an enigmatic young woman at his large estate in Connecticut. The woman, the seductive Anna Klein, is to throw Danforth's carefully ordered existence into chaos. The war in Europe is about to burst forth in all its fury and Danforth is forced to choose between his dull, regimented existence and a dangerous and exciting new life – a new life, what's more, that may even change history. The linguist Anna Klein's training involves weaponry and bomb-making, with a view (initially, at least) to assist refugees from the Spanish Civil War residing in France when the inevitable German invasion takes place. But when it becomes clear that the refugees cannot deliver the things that are expected of them, the strategy for Anna and her colleagues changes to something more concrete: nothing less than the assassination of Adolf Hitler.

There are several things that make Cook's novel so winning, not least the fact that all of this is described retrospectively after the Al Qaeda destruction of the World Trade Center, with an older Danforth telling the story to Secret Service man Paul Crane. Cutting between the two time periods (Anna Klein's story in 1939 and the terrorist atrocities of 2001), the quest that Danforth and Crane are involved in is for the truth behind Anna Klein's story – complicated by the fact that Danforth had fallen in love with her, obsessively, before her disappearance. And the uncovering of the truth here is as shocking as anything in Cook's inventive, steadily paced novel.

PATRICIA CORNWELL's *Postmortem* inaugurated her series of Kay Scarpetta novels, and surprised many when it speedily launched a legion of Scarpetta-clone female pathologists. In fact, other publishers now routinely use her name to sell their hopeful pretenders, and it was no surprise when she received the Crime Writers' Association's prestigious Dagger prize. Cornwell's books sport atmosphere and invention, and the levels of unsparing gruesomeness put down a marker that she is a match for any of her colleagues in the bloodletting stakes. Cornwell – who combines the toughness and vulnerability of her protagonist – cannily spotted that there was a need for something other than policemen or private detectives in the crime novel, but can hardly have suspected that her combination of an 'alternative profession' and a single-minded, beleaguered heroine would prove quite so groundbreaking. Scarpetta is a marvellously multifaceted creation – as deeply loved by aficionados as any protagonist in the crime field – and her bloody-minded willingness to go head to head with resentful, bullying colleagues affords a particular pleasure. But Cornwell has repeatedly said that she is well aware of the danger of staleness setting in with a series (however comfortable it may be for a writer to press all the familiar buttons), and she rings the changes in each successive Scarpetta book, notably having Kay, *persona non grata* with her ex-bosses, pursue a freelance career in Florida. Kay also struggles with a complicated relationship with her disorganised niece Lucy and her own chaotic love life. The Cornwell novels barrel along at an exhilarating pace, but the narratives have a doom-laden air, with Scarpetta exposing human venality as unerringly as she cuts into cadavers.

Cornwell's books featuring her iconic forensic sleuth have been reaching the top of the bestseller charts for years, since her debut in 1990 began what has now become a 24-book sequence. I once asked the writer how she felt about the fact that each new female claimant to her crown was announced on their book jacket as 'The Next Patricia Cornwell'; she replied, 'But I want to be the next Patricia Cornwell!' I took it to mean that she wanted to recapture some of the excitement of those early years, but she and her creation are now crime fiction institutions, with each new book expected to top – or at least match – its predecessor.

Flesh and Blood is a typical Cornwell entry. Dr Kay Scarpetta is about to set off for Miami with her FBI profiler husband Benton Wesley. She notices something curious on a wall: seven pennies.

It doesn't appear to be a child's game, as the coins are dated 1981 and appear to have been newly minted. Is it connected with a brutal killing a short distance away – a music teacher who has been shot as he took groceries from his car? Like every vacation that every sleuth has taken in every crime novel, Scarpetta's break is cut short, and she is soon on the trail of a serial sniper – one who leaves no evidence behind after his logic-defying executions. And when (as part of the case) Scarpetta investigates a shipwreck off the coast of Florida, she finds evidence that seems to draw her technologically gifted niece Lucy (the gay relative we know from other novels) into the frame.

Other writers with feminist agendas (such as Sara Paretsky) devise scenarios in which the heroine encounters frequent sexist behaviour from men, but Cornwell has a different tactic, imbuing Scarpetta with forthright, authoritative and confrontational qualities traditionally identified as male; there are no battles with sexism for Scarpetta – she's already won them. Cornwell has been criticised for the unflinching treatment of the gruesome in her novels, though one might wonder why the squeamish would pick up a novel about a forensic pathologist. This twenty-second Scarpetta novel, despite its formidable length, remains focused on its single-minded protagonists, Scarpetta and her associates (unlike James Lee Burke, Cornwell avoids state-of-the-nation novels, although Barack Obama has a walk-on part in this one); internecine conflicts in the team are as sparky as ever. Notably tenser than *Dust*, its predecessor, *Flesh and Blood* justifies its 370 pages, but its sheer bulk means that it's not one for the Patricia Cornwell novice. Aficionados, however, will be happy to immerse themselves once again in Kay Scarpetta's blood-drenched universe.

At one point, the Scarpetta books seemed to lose their momentum, and a non-Scarpetta series featuring Police Chief Judy Hammer made a negligible impact. Then the author produced a puzzlingly dotty book in *Jack the Ripper: Case Closed*, in which she staked her reputation on a Jack the Ripper solution discredited in this country years ago – that the painter Walter Sickert wielded the knife in Whitechapel. Cornwell's media appearances promoting the book combined a tetchy impatience with anyone who dared question her contentious findings with a proselytising manner that did the author no good at all.

But Cornwell's fans are prepared to forgive her such indulgences, as long as she shows that she can produce the goods in her fiction. And with *Blow Fly* (the twelfth book in the Scarpetta series), that was (largely speaking) what she managed to do – although some may find it hard to warm to this one. This outing for the resourceful medical examiner Kay Scarpetta has all the energy of the author's early work – although the levels of blood-boltered horror here make even the sanguinary excesses of the earlier books look restrained.

A woman with as much history as Scarpetta can't shake off the dust of her earlier life – and the monstrous Chandonne, a serial murderer with lycanthropic tendencies she tackled in the past, is not quite out of her life. And if this doesn't make Kay's life complicated enough, her niece Lucy, no longer in the employ of the FBI, has Chandonne's bent lawyer in her sights, with quite as murderous intentions as the serial killer had towards Kay.

As so often before, Kay is forced to juggle her personal and professional responsibilities, with her emotional life a hostage to fortune – a settled love life is not on the cards for her. What follows is a richly unsettling mélange of tortuous plotting (the above synopsis only hints at the complexity of *Blow Fly*'s multilayered narrative) and the usual full-throated bloodletting, all hurtling along at a pace that rarely gives pause for breath. Some will find certain elements here a shade overblown: the murderous sexual excesses of Chandonne's brother – who had slept with Kay – seem unconvincing and arbitrary, as if Cornwell doesn't quite trust the power of her narrative, which, God knows, is eventful enough. And when the entire structure of the plot collapses like a pack of cards after a revelation that nothing has been what it appeared to be, there's no denying that Patricia Cornwell is (knowingly or otherwise) testing the patience of her readers. And what a dark world the beleaguered Kay Scarpetta plies her trade in! Being aware of the skull beneath the skin leaves her with few illusions about the imperfections of the human race, and her bleakest prognostications about the venal actions of those she encounters – on both sides of the law – always, but always, prove chillingly accurate. But if you're the kind of crime reader who can take strong meat – and that's certainly what's on offer here – then Patricia Cornwell on something like vintage form definitely delivers the goods. Enthusiasts of cosy home counties mysteries should steer well clear!

ROBERT CRAIS may be one of the most respected and admired current American crime writers, with each new novel an eagerly awaited event, but his is no overnight success story. Crais toiled at the rock face of crime writing for many years, learning his craft on some of the most influential and seminal American TV cop shows, notably *Hill Street Blues*, *Miami Vice* and *Cagney & Lacey* (and this latter show broke almost as many rules as its more celebrated successors in the deliberately de-glamorised lives of its female cops). But Crais, like so many who have worked in the film and TV industry, began to chafe at the restrictions of the medium and the endless battles with uncomprehending executives – in this, he follows in a long and honourable line that stretches back to Raymond Chandler, whose experiences in the film industry were not happy ones. Also, like Chandler, Crais decided to utilise the delirious panoply of Los Angeles as the setting for his writing – a brave move, considering how thoroughly Chandler had colonised the city – and he began a series of novels that have made his name. *The Monkey's Raincoat* introduced readers to his sardonic private eye Elvis Cole, and with a series of ever more accomplished novels, Crais has put Cole securely in the constellation of literary detectives. His other recurring character is the hard as nails Joe Pike, an extremely useful man for Cole to have on his side. After such first-rate novels as *LA Requiem*, *Hostage* and *Demolition Angel*, Crais added to his lustre with *The Last Detective*, quite his most accomplished novel yet (even if the first few chapters don't initially exert the customary grip, despite a high-octane opening).

The American-born **DEBORAH CROMBIE** has a solid list of UK-set crime novels to her name, and her distinguishing characteristic has been her consistency; if Crombie broaches no new territory, she provides some of the most finely honed writing to be found in the genre, with nary a wasted word. *Now May You Weep* is one of her most adroit offerings: DI Gemma James accepts her friend Hazel's suggestion of a trip to the Scottish Highlands, but all is not as it seems. Gemma's secret life begins to surface. Relaxing in a small, secluded hotel, Hazel runs into her erstwhile lover Donald, who is a power in the local drinks business. But his wish that they should get together is not to be – the possibility of a reunion is shockingly terminated. Gemma finds herself digging into a grim crime and encountering a wall of suspicion and mistrust in this isolated community. A murder charge for her friend may be the least of her worries, as a deadly family rivalry comes to the surface. This is all handled with the quiet aplomb we've come to expect from Crombie, and Gemma James is one of the most sympathetic coppers in an overcrowded field, with her colleague, the doughty Duncan Kincaid, equally well drawn – their byplay is always a pleasure of the books. Not cutting-edge stuff, certainly, but a diverting 400 pages, with all the skilful plotting that marks out such Crombie novels as *And Justice There Is None* and *Dreaming of the Bones*.

Alice is a successful Manhattan businesswoman, whose love life has been chequered of late. But she is confident that things are looking up: at a wine tasting, she's met a man, Arthur, who appears to be on her wavelength – they like the same Rioja and they go to the same overpriced health clubs. Both are art lovers. Alice invites her new friend back to her apartment, where she has made some preparations in the bedroom in case the relationship develops. She casually mentions a painting she's bought, which – to her surprise – he seems to know about already. With a cold shudder, she realises that there is a man in her bedroom she doesn't really know. And then he puts on some beige cloth gloves and reaches into his pocket... One of the reasons why **JEFFERY DEAVER** is regarded as an always reliable crime writer is his skill with opening chapters (such as that described above), and after this chilling overture, *The Broken Window* puts us once again in the crotchety company of Deaver's quadriplegic forensics consultant Lincoln Rhyme.

The police have arrested a man who appears to be Alice's murderer because of a host of incriminating evidence. It's Lincoln

Rhyme's cousin, whose name is Arthur. Of course, it's a well-worn device in crime fiction to give the protagonist a personal interest in a case. But Deaver is too much the professional to slip into cliché here: Rhyme really doesn't want to get involved, and tries to persuade his colleagues that he is not going to lean on them. All of this is handled with the pace and assurance that we expect from Deaver, but the author has other tricks up his sleeve. Suddenly, we find ourselves in the consciousness of the murderer, a collector who accrues everything from meaningless street rubbish to the most significant of trophies – actual human lives. Those who have enjoyed Lincoln Rhyme's intellectual battles with highly intelligent criminals before will know just how adroit Deaver is in this territory, despite the fact that his hero is confined to a wheelchair. His legs and eyes are, of course, his colleague Amelia Sachs, who invariably finds herself in extreme danger when acting on Rhyme's hunches. Strip *The Broken Window* down to its essentials, and it's basically familiar fare – but such is Jeffery Deaver's skill that everything comes up as fresh as paint.

In *The Burning Wire*, Deaver is as skilful at keeping his literary brew fresh as in any of his earlier books (no mean trick, considering that there are nearly 30 of them). This one is something of a return to an old-fashioned, ticking-clock narrative, although Deaver keeps things up to date with a thorough-going modernity in the trappings.

New York is under siege, with the electricity grid being manipulated to murderous ends. People are dying, and suspicion falls on terrorists. But as both the CIA and the FBI sift through their fundamentalist suspects, ace criminologist Lincoln Rhyme is at work on the forensic clues, aided (as often in the past) by policewoman Amelia Sachs and a crack team including talented FBI agent Fred Dellray. It becomes clear that the crimes are not post-9/11 ideological attacks, but the work of a sinister mastermind whose cold-blooded agenda will give Rhyme and his crew their knottiest challenge yet.

The plot's the thing here, with exhilaratingly orchestrated set pieces and a host of breath-taking surprises. Ah, those Deaver surprises! No author is better at allowing us to think we've second-guessed him before pulling the rug out from beneath our feet with another narrative flourish. But does this add up to more than just a cracking (if superficial) thriller in *accelerando* mode? Actually, it does. Beneath the mechanics of the page-turning, there's some subtle psychological underpinning smuggled in by Deaver for the quadriplegic Rhyme and his foot soldiers. Nothing, mind you, that pushes things too close to more overtly serious fare, but this extra attention is a touch of 'added value' for the reader, raising the book above the penny-plain characterisation of most entries in the blockbuster thriller field.

Jeffery Deaver has recharged his batteries in the past by putting his disabled investigator on the back-burner (as with his Kathryn Dance books), but the author took on another challenge (ambitiously? foolishly?): nothing less than the mantle of 007's creator, Ian Fleming. His Bond outing, *Carte Blanche*, arrived stillborn (the fate of several post-Fleming novels), but Deaver can rest easy in the knowledge that readers will be happy to settle back into the edgy company of Rhyme and Co. – as long as he can continue to up the thriller ante with novels as nimble as *The Burning Wire*.

The perennially popular **NELSON DEMILLE** was born in New York City. His earlier books were NYPD detective novels, but his first majorly successful novel was *By the Rivers of Babylon*, published in 1978 and still in print, as are all his subsequent novels. He is a member of the Authors Guild and American Mensa, is a past president of Mystery Writers of America, and was the International Thriller Writers ThrillerMaster of the Year 2015. His lengthy catalogue includes *The Gold Coast*, *The General's Daughter*, *Night Fall*, *Wild Fire* and *The Gate House*. He also co-authored *Mayday* with Thomas Block.

The Enchanted by **RENE DENFELD** is one of those books on which a certain head of steam quickly built, suggesting that this haunting and disturbing novel was something different from the general run of crime-related novels – and so it proves to be. A prisoner sits on death row in a high-security prison; the reader is not informed of his name. A female investigator is tasked with looking into several grisly crimes, and she never sanctions a prisoner going to their death without a thorough investigation. And the prisoner himself wonders about the nature of his terrifying personality. Unusually for a novel with such a subject, there is a genuine lyricism here, which undercuts the more unsettling aspects of the narrative.

BRUCE DESILVA's crime fiction has won the Edgar and Macavity Awards; has been listed as a finalist for the Shamus, Anthony and Barry Awards; and has been published in ten foreign languages. DeSilva worked as a journalist for four decades, and his fiction has the traditional reporter's virtues of clarity and readability – *The Dread Line* is characteristic. Since being fired from his newspaper gig, ex-hack Liam Mulligan has created a new life for himself, working on both sides of the law. Liam is disturbed by the fact that someone in town is torturing animals, distracting him from a big case that needs his full attention. The New England Patriots, trying to deal with murder charges against one of their players, have hired Mulligan to investigate the background of a college star they're considering drafting, but murderous secrets emerge...

PT DEUTERMANN's first novel (after a lengthy service background) was *Scorpion in the Sea*, which gained him a contract with St Martin's Press in 1993, with whom he has published all of his successive novels. *Cold Frame* is a typical Deutermann outing. A clandestine NSA-sanctioned assassination squad, known only as DMX, goes rogue. The leader of DMX, Carl Mandeville, orchestrates the murder of one of the group's own members, who is threatening to reveal the group's existence to Congress. Pacily written fare.

A variety of his writing colleagues have been lining up to praise **PAUL DOIRON**. Tess Gerritsen described him as a powerful and evocative writer, and *Bad Little Falls* vindicates this judgement. Game warden Mike Bowditch has been sent into exile, dispatched by his superiors to a secluded outpost on the Canadian border. A blizzard hits the coast, and Mike is summoned to the remote cabin of a couple. A deranged man, half frozen, has appeared at their door saying that he has lost a friend in the storm. But this rescue mission quickly changes into a murder investigation involving a notorious drug dealer. It's no surprise that the writer CJ Box (who similarly foregrounds strikingly realised locales in his thrillers) is an admirer of this book – it's an impressive piece of work.

BARRY EISLER worked in clandestine fashion with the CIA's Directorate of Operations, then became a technology lawyer and start-up executive in Silicon Valley and Japan, earning his black belt at the Kodokan International Judo Center along the way. Eisler's fast-moving thrillers have won the Barry Award and the Gumshoe Award for best thriller of the year and have been translated into nearly 20 languages. Eisler lives in the San Francisco Bay Area and, when he's not writing novels, blogs about a variety of social issues.

What distinguishes the work of **DAVID ELLIS** (firmly in the legalistic John Grisham tradition) is a particularly apposite use of language – as in *The Hidden Man*. A summer night in the 1980s. Two-year-old Audrey Cutler is kidnapped from her bedroom, never to be seen again. Twenty years pass, and Audrey's brother Sammy has an encounter with the man the police tried to convict for her kidnapping and murder. Shortly afterwards, the abduction suspect is murdered. Sammy needs a defender and finds one in a childhood friend, Jason Kolarich. But the latter finds himself in as much dangerous trouble as the man he's defending. Keenly honed prose, always at the service of the swiftly moving narrative.

New Yorker **JT ELLISON** specialises in psychological thrillers featuring Nashville Homicide Lieutenant Taylor Jackson and medical examiner Dr Samantha Owens, and also has under her belt the Nicholas Drummond series with fellow author Catherine Coulter. Ellison is also co-host of the literary television show *A Word on Words*.

Demons have pursued the crime writer **JAMES ELLROY** since his mother was brutally murdered in 1958; in *My Dark Places*, the author – already known as a larger-than-life, eccentric figure – recounted his attempts to reopen the unsolved investigation with the help of a retired detective. That book was a searing account of self-discovery which many felt would end his creative career. That wasn't the case, although Ellroy was quoted as saying that he was through with genre fiction; however, 2014's *Perfidia* gave the lie to that statement.

The best American crime writing has always addressed key issues affecting society – class, politics and race – its sleuths moving between the various strata of US society, from the dispossessed underclass to the homes of the rich, as a detailed canvas of American class structure emerged. These penetrating examinations continue with such writers as James Lee Burke, George Pelecanos and Dennis Lehane, folding in a broader political dimension than in the past. But one writer quickly assumed pole position (albeit a *soi-disant* one); when James Ellroy calls himself 'the world's greatest crime writer', he's only half joking – and a great many people agree with him.

In 1990, *L.A. Confidential* was acclaimed as the most extraordinary crime novel produced in the US in decades. The complex narrative showcased a massive panoply of Los Angeles in the 1950s, blending a fictional scenario with real events and characters, the picture-postcard vision of the city undercut by Ellroy's anatomising of its darker side. *American Tabloid* was also much praised.

But Ellroy's winning streak was about to run dry, which is one of the reasons why each new novel is received with some trepidation, even by his admirers. *The Cold Six Thousand* was found by many to be mannered (and even unreadable), with its hyper-short sentences and minimal punctuation. Ellroy later disowned the book, but his reputation was tarnished – and *Blood's a Rover* divided readers again.

So – did Ellroy got his mojo back with the massive 700-page *Perfidia*? The book is a prequel (beginning on the day of the Japanese attack on Pearl Harbor) to the original L.A. Quartet, featuring several of the same characters and a host of real-life personalities. As before, we are presented with a richly flavoured goulash in which corrupt cops, psychopathic gangsters, Hollywood types with unorthodox sexual tastes, racists and junkies violently intersect. Police chemist Hideo Ashida is called to a gruesome ritual suicide, but he suspects mass murder. And as Japanese 'subversives' are corralled by US authorities, an orgy of bloodshed connected to Hideo's case is unleashed. Ellroy's customary command of language is overwhelming, but his recent staccato style is hiked up to cosmic levels; this is the *Finnegans Wake* of crime novels, and if you can take sentences so packed with cross-references that even basic comprehension is a challenge (though some sentences are only four words long), you'll find rich rewards. It has to be said that this is for diehard enthusiasts only; the casual reader will melt away. But at least Ellroy is still trying to expand the parameters of the crime novel – and perhaps we must pay him the compliment of cracking the prismatic (but exhilarating) prose that is his speciality.

Prior to this, there had been few books as keenly awaited as the final volume of James Ellroy's Underworld USA trilogy, *Blood's a Rover* (the title is from AE Housman), set during the incendiary period of 1968–72. As ever, we have an amazingly ambitious synthesis of crime and political chicanery, with the social mores of the day forensically examined. And all of this is delivered with the gusto we have come to expect from one of the world's most accomplished crime novelists (with, thankfully, the curiously alienating stylistic tics of the earlier *The Cold Six Thousand* – a book roundly criticised even by its creator – a distant memory). Amidst such compromised real-life characters as Richard Nixon, Ellroy focuses (in a large dramatis personae) on three protagonists: Wayne Tedrow, Jr, one of Ellroy's almost operatically off-kilter characters – a killer who numbers parricide among his many crimes and plays every side against each other with total dedication; Dwight Holly, a hard man and facilitator for J Edgar Hoover at his most sinister, who senses that the rising of Richard Nixon's star might be good for him; and Don Crutchfield, known as 'Crutch', a low-rent private eye who finds himself mired in a conspiracy reaching from the upper echelons of power to the farthest reaches of America's underclass. All of these damaged protagonists are stirred into a brew as heady as anything Ellroy has ever concocted – and the result is a state-of-the-nation (circa late 1960s/early 1970s) novel as scarifying as anything American literature has seen. *Blood's a Rover* is most definitely not for all tastes, but those who hold James Ellroy in high esteem – and there are legions who do – will be transfixed, though perhaps not elated as it's a caustic world view Ellroy serves up. The author's go-to book for most readers, however, remains the glorious, multifaceted *L.A. Confidential* (successfully filmed by Curtis Hanson). When I met Ellroy, I knew of his fearsome reputation for chewing up interviewers. The fact that I was able to hum the tune of *Perfidia* – that, and my greying temples – seemed to allow me to escape unscathed.

The UK Mantle publishing imprint has long been a guarantee of the best in crime fiction, with its celebrated no-nonsense editor Maria Rejt having the sharpest eye in the business for provocative new talent. Proof of her skills? Take, for instance, **JILL ALEXANDER ESSBAUM**, a really intriguing writer. The narrative of *Hausfrau* involves Anna Benz, outwardly living a comfortable life in an upscale area of Zurich. However, Anna, an American expat, is in a state of turmoil, alienated from her husband and his family and seeking escape in a variety of ill-advised sexual dalliances. Inevitably, her life begins to spiral out of control, and the results (as described by Essbaum) are grimly mesmerising. Apart from the storytelling grip exerted here, the author's use of language is absolutely apposite; this is a nimbly written novel.

LOREN D ESTLEMAN has been published since 1976, writing 70-plus books and many short stories. His non-fiction includes *Writing the Popular Novel*, but he is best known for his series featuring Los Angeles film detective Valentino, with such novels as *Shoot*. His lengthy Amos Walker series includes *The Sundown Speech* (the twenty-fifth in the sequence), and he has also written *The Confessions of Al Capone*. He is an authority on both criminal history and the American West and has been nominated for the National Book Award and the Mystery Writers of America's Edgar Allan Poe Award.

She's certainly not to every reader's taste, but you know you're in safe hands with the ever-reliable **JANET EVANOVICH**. In the comedy thriller stakes, she has few equals – even if, at times, her splenetic imagination falters. Not, though, with *Hard Eight*: vintage Evanovich, throwing out the one-liners in a positively spendthrift fashion. Bombshell bounty hunter Stephanie Plum is back on her Harley – so Evanovich admirers are in for another wild ride. Sardonic, and full of surprises, Evanovich's adroit thriller is crammed full of more diverting misadventures for Stephanie. As she spirals and tumbles through her customarily frenetic and incendiary world, she can hardly catch her breath, let alone her man – even if she could decide which one to chase. The author now lives in New Hampshire but (like Stephanie Plum) grew up in New Jersey and cannily utilises her background for some evocative scene-setting; the comedy and thrills are always anchored in a plausible world. She has won major crime fiction awards for her Stephanie Plum novels: *One for the Money* bagged a Crime Writers' Association Award, as did *Two for the Dough*. If you're not temperamentally disposed to Ms Plum, though, there is no easy entry point in the series. She's crime fiction Marmite.

When you are America's most celebrated prosecutor of sex crimes, a new career trajectory can be a risky business. A move into the crime fiction field, however, is exactly what **LINDA FAIRSTEIN** did, and she has been slowly building a reputation as one of the pithiest and most compelling of crime scribes around. In her previous career, Fairstein pioneered the use of DNA evidence in identifying sex offenders, along with other notable legal innovations (such as fighting the revelation of rape victims' sexual histories in court), but she would have to admit that it was harder to accomplish something so groundbreaking in her literary endeavours. *Death Dance* demonstrates that Fairstein has a fully formed grasp of narrative – even if the prose can be inelegant – and the rock-solid inside info about the legal field is pretty winning. After all, if we want more literary crime fiction, there are plenty of authors ploughing that particular furrow.

In *Bad Blood*, Assistant DA Alexandra Cooper finds herself engaged in an unusual case that will reach back into New York City's clandestine past. The defendant is a businessman, on trial for the murder of his wife. It's Cooper's job to prove that the defendant commissioned a hitman – but a sensational trial is interrupted by an even more sensational event: New York is shaken by a massive explosion in a subterranean water tunnel below the city streets. Is it terrorism, a grim accident, something to do with political corruption? And then a mysterious connection is discovered between the men who work in these dangerous tunnels and Alexandra Cooper's defendant. Soon Alex is forced into a grim underworld to exhume the putrefying corpse of a murder victim.

All of this is handled with the assurance that we now expect from Fairstein, and if her heroine is cut from very familiar cloth, she's a persuasive character. What makes *Bad Blood* rise effortlessly above the other legal thrillers clogging the shelves is the masterful treatment of the city's tunnel workers: the sandhogs are almost like a secret society, men holding down a highly dangerous job – one with a rigorously maintained set of rules, along with feuds whose consequences can be deadly. It's the treatment of this element that makes this one of Fairstein's most edgy novels.

CHRISTA FAUST grew up in New York City, in the Bronx and Hell's Kitchen. She has said that she worked in the city's Times Square peep booths and later as a fetish model and professional dominatrix. She sold her first short story when she moved to Los Angeles in the early 1990s, and her subsequent novels such as *Money Shot* and *Choke Hold* have demonstrated an unorthodox and uncompromising talent.

ROBERT FERRIGNO was born in Florida, growing up on the last paved street of a small town: 'Spending my youth,' he said, 'cutting secret passages through the palmetto thickets with a machete and occasionally burning down those palmettos for the simple pleasure of seeing the fire trucks arrive, sirens blaring.' Later, he became 'a full-time gambler' living in a high-crime area populated by 'starving artists, alcoholics and petty criminals'. His novels have enjoyed enthusiastic acclaim, notably his thriller *Prayers for the Assassin*, in which religious extremists control the US. In the north, veiled women are now the majority, alcohol is banned and mosques flourish, while the southern Bible Belt remains unbendingly Christian. Religious edicts are absolute law, and rebels dream of regaining the right to free will.

DAN FESPERMAN is the real deal, a writer of literary bent in terms of complexity and ambition, whose remarkable accomplishment is demonstrated in such books as *The Arms Maker of Berlin*. In that novel, the placid academic life enjoyed by Nat Turnbull is interrupted when his ex-colleague, Gordon Wolfe, is arraigned for purloining secret documents relating to the Second World War. Nat is forced to examine FBI archives, and learns about an enigmatic student resistance group called the White Rose. The way in which Fesperman handles multifarious plotlines is quite as authoritative as one would expect from the author of books such as *The Prisoner of Guantánamo* (perhaps the best Fesperman novel for the novice). It goes without saying, of course, that the writer is a master of the orchestration of tension – but he is equally good at characterising his vulnerable, conflicted protagonists.

Heard of the American writer **JOSEPH FINDER**? He may not have the name recognition of some of his peers, but those very peers line up to praise his abilities on the jacket of *The Fixer*, with encomiums from heavyweights Michael Connelly, Tess Gerritsen and Lisa Gardner. Journalist Rick Hoffman is abruptly bumped by his magazine and left penniless. But he still has the keys to his absent father's house, and discovers – hidden in the walls – millions of dollars. Rick is well aware that spending the money without knowing where it came from may be a bad mistake. And his father, who has lost the ability to speak, can't tell him just how much danger he's in. Things – inevitably – get very nasty. This is Finder at the top of his game, with the kind of orchestration of suspense that guarantees a one- or two-sitting read.

Similarly accomplished were the earlier *Paranoia* and (among its successors) *Power Play*, which finally brought the author – after several earlier books – the acclaim (and sales) that were his due. The secret was out. No more was Finder a name to be whispered in adulatory tones among admirers; interest had begun to spread far afield. His Cold War thrillers take us into the darker recesses of the CIA and the KGB, but, like le Carré, Finder is also more than capable of dealing with the post-Cold War world, as the excellent *Paranoia* demonstrates. *Company Man* is almost equally good, melding brilliantly orchestrated suspense with characterisation that has the richness of the best literary fiction. Nick Conover has a blue-collar background but has succeeded as the head of a large corporation in a company town. But Nick is now cordially loathed, having played a part in swingeing company layoffs. When Nick's family is menaced by a mysterious stalker, he finds himself very quickly at the end of his tether: somebody is dead, and Nick is in the frame. The only way to extricate himself is to begin a massive investigation into his own company. If the modern thriller has a future beyond thick-ear action or globetrotting, faceless thrillers with Old Masters in the title, it would be nice to think that Finder is the man to inaugurate this new era.

Before the amazing international success of *Gone Girl*, **GILLIAN FLYNN** was as much a contradiction as the vulnerable heroine of her debut novel, *Sharp Objects*. Flynn claimed to this writer to be 'white trash from the hog capital of America' – but she is actually a well-spoken, sharply dressed journalist (TV critic for US magazine *Entertainment Weekly*), both of whose parents are academics. *Sharp Objects* features journo Camille Preaker, who similarly calls herself 'white trash from old money', and her plausibility is no doubt due to the dual traits of her creator – though one hopes that Flynn has a better relationship with her mother than the poisonous one between Camille and her neurotic, hypochondriac parent. The book arrived in the UK festooned with plaudits from such masters of the thriller as Stephen King – but so do many other novels. Does this one live up to the hype? Actually, it does – and, more than that, Flynn has created something fresh (if that's the word) in this steamy synthesis of Southern Gothic, literary character study and Oprah Winfrey-style grossly behaving working-class Americans. We're hooked from Chapter 1, in which the journalist heroine, ill at ease with herself and her job on a bottom-of-the-barrel newspaper, is summoned by her editor, who makes it clear that she never quite lived up to the hopes he had for her. So when he suggests she return to her home town of Wind Gap, Missouri, to write about the abduction and murder of two young girls, she feels obliged to go, despite her better judgement. Camille may be from one of the most moneyed families in the town, but the sprawling Victorian mansion that is her home is where she knows she'll find her demanding mother – and only being in a different city has allowed her to attain some kind of mental equilibrium. And there's her slutty half-sister, a desperately precocious 13-year-old who has an entourage of Goth teenage girlfriends and some kind of hold over the town. Back with her estranged mother, Camille is once again caught up in a childhood tragedy that has left her scarred – and while identifying with the murdered girls, she begins to make the wrong decisions: she has sex with the investigator assigned to the case, and even beds the prime suspect, a troubled teenager. All of this is dispatched in fascinating fashion, more Southern Gothic à la daytime trash TV than William Faulkner. And there's a jaw-dropping twist that you may not see coming...

However pleased Gillian Flynn may have been with respectable sales and enthusiastic reviews for her earlier books, nothing could have prepared her for the prodigious success that was to follow the publication of her novel *Gone Girl*. Like many of my journalistic colleagues, I calmly welcomed the book on its appearance in 2012 as a typically ingenious Flynn thriller, a book satisfyingly wrong-footing the reader and creating an acidulous picture of a marriage where nothing is what it seems to be – the key book, in fact, of the recent 'domestic noir' trend. But none of us expected the phenomenon that was the book and the subsequent Ben Affleck/Rosamund Pike film (nor, I suspect, did her publishers), moving Flynn very firmly from somewhere above the midlist to the upper echelons of crime fiction success. Her problem then became not just to spend the humungous amount of money that *Gone Girl* has placed in her bank account, but to follow up a book that became almost a cultural sensation in its own right. But Gillian Flynn is a talented enough writer to do just that.

GM FORD has led quite a life. Ford is Gerry to his friends, though not to his readers – it is, he says, the name of an accident-prone ex-US president and perhaps isn't quite right for a crime novelist. His books are solid entertainment: tough, yes, but shot through with humanity and humour. And, one by one, they are building up a laser-lit picture of modern American society that sports a fascinating mix of his experience of everything from the drug-fuelled sexual wonderland of the 1960s to the dangerous, socially alienating world of the modern metropolis. For 20 years, Ford taught creative writing to high school and college students, before deciding it was time to do some serious creative writing of his own. As an aficionado of detective fiction (about which Ford is inordinately passionate), he created his own tenacious Seattle private eye, Leo Waterman, but after six well-received books that did not necessarily perform spectacularly, Ford felt that he was on a plateau and that he should move on – and, understandably, he wanted a breakthrough that would have more of an impact on readers.

And he did it – with a bang. Ford's gumshoe Leo Waterman was granted a temporary vacation; and, in 2001, Ford produced a much more gritty novel with *Fury*, a powerful and involving serial killer mystery (borrowing the title of a Fritz Lang film) that kick-started the career of an abrasive new anti-hero, journalist/true crime writer Frank Corso. Ford told me that 'Corso is my alter ego. My last protagonist was a nicer person than he is, kind and understanding. Not Corso! And with such a determined hero, the narratives can be really astringent – though these are still obliquely feel-good fiction, in that the bad guy is usually satisfyingly dealt with and justice is seen to be done (unlike, all too often, the real world).'

Sometimes a crime writer comes along who shakes the genre so that all the clichés come rattling out like loose nails, leaving something clean and spare. **TOM FRANKLIN** proved to be such a writer with *Crooked Letter, Crooked Letter*, an atmospheric crime offering set in rural Mississippi. But is Franklin even a crime writer at all? Or is he, like his great predecessor William Faulkner (a clear influence), using the trappings of the crime novel for literary ends?

In rural Mississippi, Larry Ott and Silas Jones were once friends; Larry came from a lower-middle-class white background, while Silas was the son of a poor black single mother. When, however, a teenage girl vanished after a date with Larry, the friendship ended. Years pass, and Silas is now the town's only police officer, while Larry is an alienated individual who has never shaken off the suspicion that he abducted the missing girl. This intriguing premise is handled by Franklin with great assurance, and fully justifies all the praise that the novel received when it appeared. So authoritative was this earlier (solo) book that the heart sank when we saw that he had enlisted his wife (poet Beth Ann Fennelly) as co-writer for *The Tilted World*, but this unruly tale set against the historic flooding of the Mississippi River is even more impressive than *Crooked Letter*. Two incorruptible Prohibition-era federal agents are sent to investigate the disappearance of two colleagues who had been closing in on a local bootlegger. Gritty, vivid fare.

American writer **BRIAN FREEMAN** has long been recognised as one of the most able practitioners of the locale-specific thriller genre, and *Season of Fear* joins its solid predecessors as another in the reliable line of novels by Freeman. A grim tropical storm is heading towards the Florida coast, but the state itself is experiencing another storm – a political one, affecting the upper echelons of power. The principal candidate for governor, Diane Fairmont, has received a worrying death threat – one that threatens to repeat a massacre from a decade earlier. Detective Cab Bolton finds himself obliged to tackle trouble in a variety of forms.

KINKY FRIEDMAN is one of the quirkiest and most original writers working in what might loosely be called the crime genre. His unorthodox plotting, unique characters and (most of all) cheerfully black humour mark out his work as quite unlike that of any other practitioner. *The Mile High Club* is one of his most demented offerings, with his protagonist (curiously, also called Kinky) up against a series of mystifying problems. Meeting a beautiful woman on a plane, Kinky finds himself holding her pink imitation leather suitcase when she suddenly disappears. But is he fated to meet the beguiling Khadija Kejela again? Soon, Friedman's bemused hero is mixed up with Arab terrorists, Israeli counter-agents and sinister State Department officials all mixing it in Kinky's Vandam Street loft in search of passports missing from that pink leather suitcase. And the one area in which Friedman pays tribute to his illustrious literary predecessors is in his treatment of his alluring femme fatale: Khadija is, of course, not what she seems to be, and Kinky will rue the day he met her – not least when he's abducted by ruthless Islamic terrorists. As usual, the first-person narration is impeccably handled, with the one-liners delivered with customary aplomb. If the freshness of earlier Kinkster outings isn't present, there's the pleasure of spending time with an old friend – and Friedman is someone it's always good to meet up with again. Best of all, he's able to juxtapose the laughs and the thrills with a masterly hand – an area in which so many writers come unstuck.

Generally speaking, authors hate categorisation – they like to think that they're writing novels that don't lend themselves to easy labels. Conversely, bookshops like categorisation – after all, booksellers have to file all these damned books somewhere. But what about readers? To categorise or not to categorise? If the truth be told, most of us like a little guidance, particularly with a writer new to us. So where do we file the American writer **ALAN FURST**? Literary novel? Espionage? Historical fiction?

Furst's *Kingdom of Shadows* invoked glowing comparisons with Graham Greene; his idiosyncratic recreation of 1930s Europe in the run-up to World War Two has the richness and authenticity that only the best writers can boast. That novel deals with the growing tide of fascism in Europe, and represents a new vigour for the espionage tale. *Blood of Victory* has the same trenchant scene-setting and felicitous grasp of character as its predecessor. The setting is once again wartime Europe, and it's the territory to which Furst returns in *The Foreign Correspondent* (Furst's cheeky appropriation of a famous Hitchcock title is misleading – this is a far darker piece than Hitch's *jeu d'esprit*). In fact, the book is set in the feverish period just before the Second World War; the eponymous foreign correspondent is Carlo Weisz of Reuters, covering the final campaign of the Spanish Civil War. But a double death at a Paris hotel (a favourite spot for clandestine sexual liaisons) propels him into a new job. The victims are the editor of émigré newspaper *Liberazione* and his lover – both have been murdered by OVRA, the secret police of Mussolini's fascist regime. Carlo, seduced by the laudable ideology and the romance of the idea, unwisely agrees to take over editorship of the paper – and puts himself in a dangerous position. But it's equally dangerous to rekindle an old affair in Berlin with intriguing Christa, now married to a rich older man. As Carlo becomes the target of the murderous agents of OVRA, the French Sûreté and even British Intelligence, political imperatives assume second place to the task of simply staying alive.

Furst is an American author who considers himself European, and his lineage as a writer stretches right back to Joseph Conrad, although he can, disappointingly, deal in national stereotypes. A Hooray Henry Englishman called Geoffrey Sparrow, given to 'toothy har-hars', is a reminder that we're not reading Greene, who would have balanced the character with other Englishmen presented in more rounded fashion. But, once again, *The Foreign Correspondent* is a reminder that the espionage novel (if that's what we're going to call this) can still be a vehicle for fine writing, and Furst's audacious reinvention of the genre is a constant delight.

Stephen King did not necessarily do **MG GARDINER** (aka Meg Gardiner) a favour when he anointed her as a future superstar of the thriller genre: despite her first-rate novels, it took her a while to make a breakthrough commensurate with her talents. But then she appeared with a new publisher, a newly abbreviated moniker, and her best book so far, *The Shadow Tracer*. Her heroine, Sarah, is living quietly with her five-year-old daughter Zoe, but then she hears that the school bus has crashed. When Sarah arrives at the hospital, her life is changed irrevocably. Although Zoe is uninjured, it is revealed that she is actually Sarah's niece, and her mother, Beth, died at the hands of a malign cult. What's more, the little girl possesses an even more dangerous secret. As ever with Gardiner, we are ineluctably drawn into the desperate plight of the heroine, and the orchestration of tension is accomplished.

Her publishers may hope that a new name will make Gardiner a more commercial proposition; her talent, however, needs no finessing. More proof? The similarly accomplished *The Burning Mind*, in which the new moniker hardly signals a change, although the novels appear to be getting longer; this one weighs in at nearly 500 pages. But if anything is new, it is, surprisingly, an even more assured sense of authority, recognised in a jacket encomium by Usual Suspect Stephen King, who compares Gardiner to Lee Child and Michael Connelly. Harper Flynn is left near to death when the club in LA she works at is the scene of an assault by raiders wearing masks. Struggling to come to terms with her life after the trauma of the incident, she is haunted by the thought that not only did one of the attackers escape, but the survivors of the brutal attack are now in the firing line of a ruthless killer or killers – and it is only a matter of time before her name comes up. She meets scepticism, but one man believes her: Sheriff Aiden Garrison. However, for reasons of his own, he is not the best possible ally she could have. As in the earlier *The Shadow Tracer*, there is a storytelling ethos at work here that fully justifies the oldest cliché in the reviewer's lexicon: this one is unputdownable.

'When you wake up in a dark wooden box, you'll tell yourself this isn't happening. You'll push against the lid, of course. No surprise there. You'll beat at the sides with your fists, pummel your heels against the bottom… and you'll scream.' No, not a passage from Edgar Allan Poe's 'The Premature Burial', but the arresting opening of a typical **LISA GARDNER** offering, *Find Her*, which effortlessly overcomes the problems of an overcomplicated plot to deliver psychological crime writing of the first order.

The central character is Flora Dane, who, to all appearances, has survived a horrifying ordeal when she was abducted on holiday in Florida seven years previously by a truck driver. Jacob Ness was a sadist who subjected her to a repeated torment, confining her to a coffin for most of the 472 days of her captivity – when she wasn't being forced to have sex with him. After her release, dealing with the trauma that has scarred her life, she has become adept at self-defence and has acquired an obsessive interest in kidnapped women and the problems of survival. As the narrative progresses (and it is delivered with the sense of pace that is one of Lisa Gardner's trademarks), she becomes a kind of one-woman anti-kidnapping machine, lethal to criminals. Until she once again vanishes, which draws her to the attention of Gardner's series character Detective DD Warren.

The quality of crime writing on offer today ranges from the indifferent through the workmanlike to the genuinely inventive, and Gardner is firmly in the upper range of the last category. She has demonstrated in such early books as *The Other Daughter* and *The Perfect Husband* that she's more than capable of delivering the genuine article: thrillers always couched in smart, well-turned prose. *The Third Victim* is equally strong, with a grim crime tearing apart a town. But is *Find Her* in that impressive company? Not quite – but if this isn't one of the very best Gardner offerings, there are perhaps a couple of reasons: an implausibly lengthy series of kidnappings, and the split narrative between the detective and the kidnapped Flora. The former doesn't always maintain an equal balance of interest, with Flora's sequences inevitably more powerful, if a touch repetitive. But Gardner is too accomplished a writer to seriously loosen her grip on the reader, and, caveats aside, *Find Her* often channels that storytelling authority that is her ace in the hole.

For three decades, the American writer **ELIZABETH GEORGE** has demonstrated that she is the ultimate Anglophile, setting her novels in the UK. But she has repeatedly shown her surprise at the power of the English tabloids and has noted that when she presents their behaviour in outrageous terms, the real-life equivalents will always outdo her fictional versions. The red tops, in fact, are central to *Just One Evil Act*, which is George's *War and Peace*, at least in terms of length (an imposing 700-odd pages). But this is no mere indulgence, as the author has considerably broadened her range in terms of setting (a vividly drawn Italy) and has even introduced an intriguing new character, the saturnine Inspector Salvatore Lo Bianco. It's clear, too, that George finds the Italian police and judicial system bizarre, and dropping Inspector Thomas Lynley into this milieu is a clever touch.

While Lynley struggles to deal with the death of his wife Helen, DS Barbara Havers moves centre stage. The daughter of a close friend and neighbour of Barbara's disappears in London in the company of her mother. Hadiyyah, the young girl, reappears five months later and is kidnapped from an open-air market in Lucca. Scotland Yard is reluctant to get involved, until Barbara realises that by finessing the most unscrupulous of the British tabloids she can bring about an investigation. The Amanda Knox trial is clearly part of the DNA of the narrative here, and George has spoken of the prurient frenzy with which the British tabloids settled on Knox as the villain: the whole 'Foxy Knoxy' syndrome. But it is not Barbara who is sent to Italy; rather, her superior officer DI Lynley is obliged to cope with language problems, racial issues and even the bloody-mindedness of an Italian magistrate desperate to put somebody – anybody – in the frame for the crime.

The new elements here have clearly had an energising effect on

George's work, which, while not slipping into repetition, had recently lost some of its original freshness. Her treatment of the Mediterranean settings – along with a raft of intriguing new characters, such as a seedy investigator – shows a new exuberance. The prodigious sprawl of the book will perhaps rule it out for any casual readers, but George aficionados will consider that *Just One Evil Act* possesses (as Schumann said of Schubert) 'heavenly length'.

What does the crime writer **TESS GERRITSEN** have in common with Clint Eastwood? Apart, that is, from being a massively successful purveyor of entertaining popular culture? In order to buy studio funding for his more personal projects, Eastwood would periodically turn out a crowd-pleasing, all-stops-out thriller that focused on suspense rather than character – and that appears to be what the highly talented Gerritsen has done in *Keeping the Dead* (even though such a trade-off with her publishers would hardly have been necessary – her seamless blend of good writing and pulse-racing tension has long been her stock-in-trade, so no artificial division between serious and popular books was ever on the cards for her).

This novel is markedly more linear and less character-driven than her usual fare, but perhaps it's none the worse for that. All of the customary page-turning skills that distinguished such earlier Gerritsen books as *The Mephisto Club* and *The Bone Garden* are profusely in evidence, and the plotting remains as assured as ever – but those who love her work may wish she'd found time for more character development (absolutely *de rigueur* in earlier books) for her much-loved series heroines, forensic anthropologist Maura Isles and detective Jane Rizzoli.

That's not to say that individual character detail isn't on offer here, but it's delivered very much on the hoof, as Rizzoli and Isles barely draw breath when investigating a particularly grisly and arcane murder mystery. A media rumpus has erupted at Pilgrim Hospital, as a dead woman is given an X-ray, with Maura Isles in attendance. The woman has been dead for centuries – the subject is a mummy. And when – to the amazement of everyone present – a bullet is discovered in the body, Maura calls on her long-time associate Detective Jane Rizzoli to register a homicide. The spotlight is thrown on a venerable family-owned museum, where, behind a false wall, gruesome finds are made; it becomes apparent that the two women are up against a psychopath, a killer who is playing elaborate games for his own obscure purposes. As revelation follows revelation, it's clear that Tess Gerritsen has the mechanics of the crime and thriller genre at her fingertips. Interestingly, there is a more overt feminist slant here than in Gerritsen's earlier books – a slant that is probably more persuasive than more directly male-hostile polemics. Both heroines – secure at the top of their professions – are far more capable and resourceful than any of the variously venal, stupid or criminal males they encounter; Jane Rizzoli even admonishes her colleague Barry Frost about an ill-advised, hormone-led sexual attraction – she's right, of course. Finally though, what counts is Gerritsen's unassailable skill at delivering visceral, invigorating entertainment.

It's difficult to come up with something fresh in the thriller genre, which by now has exhausted most concepts. But with his kinetic debut *Volk's Game*, **BRENT GHELFI** has done just that. His tough protagonist is Russian gangster Alexei Volkovoy, moving through a colourfully realised Moscow, with dangerous encounters on every street corner. Volkovoy is a veteran from Russia's Chechnyan war, now doing shady black market deals while simultaneously getting his hands dirty for the Russian military. Commissioned to steal a lost da Vinci masterpiece (note the obligatory Leonardo reference – no harm in going for the Dan Brown market). The resourceful Volkovoy is soon followed by a wide array of nemeses, baying for his blood. Little subtlety here, but much vivid scene-setting and breathlessly orchestrated action set pieces. The recipe for a bestseller, in fact.

A typical **JOHN GILSTRAP** novel? How about *Even Steven*? Gilstrap has produced some strong thrillers, with *At All Costs* an important book for the author, and the gusto of that novel is echoed in *Even Steven*, which marries the suspense with subtler themes, such as human longing. The Martins, Bobby and Susan, have one keen wish: to have a child of their own. While considering how their marriage could be consolidated by such a gift, the couple undertake a camping trip, little realising that this will utterly change their lives. An unkempt, dirty young boy, shivering with cold, appears at their campsite, and the Martins' parental urges are soon kicking in. But when the boy's kidnappers make a violent appearance, the couple are caught up in the savage killing of a police officer. Soon they are outrunning a band of dangerous criminals, and, while struggling to stay alive, dark emotions concerning their failed pregnancies add a disturbing spin to the situation. Gilstrap has managed a dual achievement here: ace storytelling as ever, but he has also channelled a notion once very popular in the thriller genre – the action takes place over the course of 24 hours, and Gilstrap maintains the tension effortlessly with his ticking-clock scenario.

The Perk is a substantial thriller (weighing in at nearly 500 pages), and a reminder that **MARK GIMENEZ** is one of the most able practitioners of the legal thriller at work today. Comparisons with John Grisham throughout his career have been many (and inevitable) – something he told me he didn't object to – but there are those who are now daring to whisper that Gimenez is becoming a better writer. After the death of his wife, city lawyer Beck Hardin returns to the town in Texas where he grew up, and finds it an attractive place, very different from the pressured cities he's worked in. But this is a small town with its own particular problems – notably an unsolved case that turns out to be the most dangerous Beck has ever worked on.

MELISSA GINSBURG's first novel, *Sunset City*, accrued some prestigious supporters, from Megan Abbott to Nic Pizzolatto, creator of *True Detective* – and, what's more, the authoritative Sarah Weinman called it 'my favourite crime fiction debut of 2016'. *Sunset City* is an erotic, heat-drenched piece that evokes the atmosphere of Ginsburg's native Houston with great vividness – she finds possibilities in Houston that an earlier generation unearthed in Los Angeles. And her command of language and images, not to mention her sharp observation of human nature, really resonates. It's also (praise be!) refreshingly concise.

The word has been building on **WILLIAM GIRALDI**, with a host of enthusiasts providing encomiums – including such gifted cult writers as Daniel Woodrell and Thomas McGuane. And after finishing the economical, perfectly judged literary thriller *Hold the Dark*, most readers will feel that the fuss is justified. The setting is the Alaskan tundra, and the book is both an unsettling journey into human darkness and a disquisition on betrayal. Three children have been taken from an isolated Alaskan village by wolves, and Russell Core, an expert on predatory animals, arrives to look into the killings – but he discovers a sinister skein of human malfeasance. *The Hero's Body* is a memoir from Giraldi; smart and profound, it is a gripping meditation on what it means to 'be a man' in contemporary society.

VICTOR GISCHLER may have written an accomplished fantasy trilogy recently, but the writer's admirers may prefer his first novel, *Gun Monkeys*, which was nominated for an Edgar Award. His *Shotgun Opera* was an Anthony Award finalist, while his fifth novel, the quirky *Go-Go Girls of the Apocalypse*, enjoyed a strong following. Another iron in his fire is comics writing, including the tough *The Punisher: Frank Castle* and *Deadpool*.

JAMES GRADY was born in Shelby, Montana, a tough oil field, railroad and farming town clinging to the prairie 60 miles east of the Rocky Mountains, a half-hour drive south of Canada, and (as he says) 'a million miles from everywhere else'. At 24, while living in a converted garage in Missoula, he sold his signature novel, *Six Days of the Condor*, before working as an investigative reporter, covering politics, crime, drug trafficking and espionage. For his novels, Grady has been an Edgar nominee, while France awarded him the Grand Prix du Roman Noir (2001) and Italy gave him the Raymond Chandler Award (2003). Grady aficionados rate his novel *Mad Dogs* among his most distinctive work, and the book received Japan's Baka-Misu literary award in 2008. While working on a Hollywood project, he wrote a sequel to *Six Days of the Condor*, *Last Days of the Condor*.

Two of the queens of crime writing in the US are Patricia Cornwell and **SUE GRAFTON**. While Cornwell (who writes grisly, narrative-driven novels full of uncompromising forensic detail) is, in person, intense and somewhat prickly, Sue Grafton – who was the Trojan horse for women crime writers in the States – is softly spoken and unostentatious. While there is a distinct change of atmosphere when the starry Cornwell enters the room, Grafton would pride herself on the fact that she might not be noticed. It's her combination of a laser-sharp ability to read (and reproduce) human behaviour while not giving too much away about herself that Grafton has parlayed into her long-running female private eye series, which began in 1982 with *A is for Alibi* and has almost got to the end of the alphabet – at the time of writing, we were awaiting publication of *Y is for...* While the adjective 'feisty' is routinely applied to Cornwell's pathologist heroine Kay Scarpetta, Grafton's gumshoe Kinsey Millhone does not lend herself so readily to easy categorisation. While undoubtedly a survivor, and preternaturally gifted in getting under the skins of those she encounters, Kinsey has a chameleon-like skill that helps put her witnesses and suspects at ease, very often so that they will betray themselves. In this, she is something like an American distaff George Smiley, with an added taste for junk food and rather more changes of brassiere.

S is for Silence demonstrates why Grafton has such a dedicated following, with Kinsey Millhone as dogged (and perceptive) as ever, trying to crack a particularly intractable mystery. In July 1953, the promiscuous Violet (married to the abusive Foley) disappeared, driving off in her new Chevy, blowing a kiss to her daughter. Thirty-five years later, that daughter, the unhappy Daisy, has decided that finding out what happened to her mother is the only way she can put her own unresolved life in order. She hires Kinsey, who questions all those who knew Violet before her disappearance. Was she murdered by the brutal Foley? Or is the reason behind her vanishing a more complex affair? As Kinsey gets closer to the truth she finds the easy cooperation of the townspeople hardening into something more hostile, and the slashing of her car tyres is the first sign that things will turn very nasty.

Grafton eschews the synthetic climaxes that other, lesser writers inject into their narratives to add spurious excitement, and provides a more steady and realistic unravelling of the central mystery. If there's a problem with that approach here, it's possibly the fact that Kinsey is told over and over again how sluttish the missing Violet was, and any description of the latter's husband is incomplete without the information that he used to beat her. But just as we're getting impatient, Grafton cannily moves things on to another level, and the revelations begin to come satisfyingly thick and fast. Like her great predecessor Ross Macdonald, Grafton foregrounds idiosyncratic characterisation at all times, and some of the observation of small-town American life here has the acuity of Richard Ford.

SARA GRAN's novels include *Dope*, *Come Closer*, *Saturn's Return to New York*, and the Claire DeWitt series. Her books have been published in over a dozen countries and as many languages. She also writes for TV and film. Born and raised in Brooklyn, she now lives in California.

After some success with *Ravens*, **GEORGE DAWES GREEN** has struggled to find as commercial a follow-up. The protagonists of that much talked-about thriller, Shaw and Romeo, find themselves at a convenience store in Georgia. The store is one from which a multimillion dollar jackpot ticket has been sold – and when the clerk reveals the identity of the winning family, Shaw hits upon an outrageous scheme. He and Romeo take the family hostage, with a regime of fear their weapon. But as the pressure mounts, the situation becomes incendiary. This is the kind of crime fiction writing to persuade those not sold on the genre that it offers one of the most compelling of reading experiences – even if Green now seems a tad adrift.

To the casual reader of crime and thriller novels, **JOHN GRISHAM** is a copper-bottomed promise of reliable storytelling acumen and authentic-seeming legal shenanigans. *The Summons*, for instance, is pretty much standard Grisham fare: written in straightforward, unadorned prose, but sporting a plausible, engrossing plot that makes up in sheer page-turning stickiness what it might lack in sophistication. Ironically, the central conceit echoes Jonathan Franzen's *The Corrections*: two dysfunctional brothers living unsatisfactory lives in the shadow of their withholding, bone-headed father. The eponymous summons requests that the brothers (alienated law professor Ray and wastrel Forrest, a walking cocktail of addictions) travel to their reclusive father's forbidding home in Clanton, Mississippi for a final settling of the dying ex-judge's estate. But a life-changing shock awaits both brothers – and Ray finds himself dealing with a fortune he finds barely hidden in the judge's house. Is it dirty money? Before long, Ray is looking over his shoulder at a sinister stranger closing in on the money and struggling to deal with the downward spiral of his brother's life. Grisham's style is as economical as ever – flat exposition is tempered with the storyteller's glittering eye that holds us inexorably. Characterisation is serviceable, and Ray is more complex and conflicted than most of the authors' protagonists, although the drug-and-drink ingesting Forrest is little more than the sum of his addictions. There's no sex, of course, and virtually no violence – Grisham has railed against the excesses of Hollywood in these areas. However, in what seems like a reaction to the author's much-trumpeted born-again Christianity, religion is given very short shrift in *The Summons* – sanctimonious preachers are characterised as having little sympathy for the civil rights movement. Stylistically, this is as unambitious as ever – such lines as 'she was an ageing tart, but still an active volcano' may cause the spirits to fall – but Grisham enthusiasts will feel they've got their money's worth – particularly as the legal trappings here are as persuasive as ever.

In *The Confession*, Travis Boyette cannot believe his luck. He is a man guilty of a vicious crime who has managed to escape justice, relishing his good fortune even as an innocent man languishes in prison. In 1998, in the whistle-stop city of Sloan in East Texas, Boyette abducted a young high-school cheerleader, a girl who was very popular with her fellow students. After raping her, Boyette strangled her and buried her body – and buried it in such a way that she will never be found. The murderer realises that any chance that he will be convicted of the crime recedes when local football star Donté Drumm becomes the focus of attention for police and prosecutors. Found guilty of the crime, Drumm is sentenced to death. Nearly ten years pass, and the real killer is arrested for a different crime, but subsequently paroled. The innocent man, however, is still on death row, with just days to go before he is to be executed. But he has one ray of hope that he doesn't know about – the real criminal, Boyette, is dying from an inoperable brain tumour and undergoes an uncharacteristic attack of conscience. He decides to tell the police that he is the murderer. But time is short – perhaps too short to stop the judicial killing of an innocent man.

John Grisham is, of course, celebrated for his peerless legal thrillers, and in that field he has few equals – pretenders to his throne are routinely, and hopefully, compared to Grisham on their dust jackets. But while Grisham never forgets that he is primarily a popular entertainer, it's clear that issues of wrongful conviction have been playing on his mind for some time. He has talked about the many real-life miscarriages of justice that have inspired *The Confession*. In fact, Grisham is the public face of an initiative called 'The Innocence Project', an organisation whose aim is to use DNA evidence and testing to ensure the release of people who have been erroneously convicted of crime. But readers need not worry; Grisham has not written a tract with this book – he is too canny a writer to allow any axe-grinding to get in the way of the narrative. If the customary Grisham tension is reined in here rather than screwed as tight as in such books as *The Summons*, there is the usual storytelling muscle to match the authorial anger that inspired the novel.

ANDREW GROSS's *The One Man* was submitted for consideration for the 2017 Crime Writers' Association's Ian Fleming Steel Dagger, and proved to be a considerable find. With this remarkable thriller, Gross overcame the daunting hurdle of being known as a soldier in the army of co-writers for James Patterson, whose donkey work he did on several books before penning a solo outing, *The Blue Zone*, under his own name. The British crime pundit Ali Karim was an early UK proselytiser for *The One Man* and told me he found it 'truly astonishing – a huge departure from his very well-written and slick "airport thrillers", though it has a tenuous link to his James Patterson collaboration *The Jester*.'

The futuristic thriller is a genre once largely colonised by the late Michael Crichton, and, latterly, Michael Marshall, both of whose names are invoked in *Wicker*, an intriguing debut for **KEVIN**

GUILFOILE. The hot topic of cloning is the plot engine here: society in Guilfoile's novel treats cloned babies as an acceptable option for infertile couples, but fundamentalist religious groups are ruthlessly determined to terminate the practice. Davis Moore is a specialist in the cloning industry, trying to deal with the murder of his daughter. While the killer goes free, Moore finds himself with access to the criminal's DNA – and decides to produce a clone so that he can confront his daughter's murderer. But what will the boy, Justin, become? This fascinating premise – a genuinely innovative one – is handled with cool and persuasive assurance by a skilled writer.

A recurrent theme with **JAMES HALL**'s recalcitrant detective Thorn has been his steadfast spurning of Florida society, but in *Blackwater Sound*, Thorn is in the thick of it. He encounters beguiling police photographer Alexandra Rafferty, and sparks begin to fly – along with the customary violent action. However, Hall has never been interested in the clichés of the thriller genre, so this isn't just an example of 'meeting cute' set against a plot crammed with menace and suspense. As with the finest writers in the genre, Hall is well aware that, from Raymond Chandler onwards, it's been essential to paint your locale quite as vividly as you can – and Florida is richly detailed here, in all its gaudy, chaotic (and blackly comic) splendour. And with this requirement so comfortably taken care of, Hall can indulge in the central plot, involving Alexandra's father, who is beginning to suffer from something like senile dementia. And as Rafferty Sr is the grandfather of two of the more sinister characters in the novel, Thorn is – as usual – quickly up to his armpits in trouble. Hall's novels have always thrived on coincidences: the number of times Thorn stumbles over corpses could give even Philip Marlowe pause for thought, but who cares? The villainy here takes in the usual corruption themes, but stirs in some elements that seem to belong to the science fiction field – but delivered with such aplomb that we feel no shifting of gears. Thorn is always a reliable protagonist, but the winning stroke here is bad girl Morgan Braswell, in thrall to a vanished incestuous passion from the past; she's a strongly detailed character – and more persuasive than her psychotic brother, who is characterised along familiar lines. The violence is dispatched with the panache we expect from Hall, and while this may not be the author at his most incisive (you have to go to *Rough Draft* for that), it's still a heady and flavoursome mix.

TIM HALLINAN wrote a six-book series set in LA in the 1990s. He also launched the popular Bangkok-set Poke Rafferty series in 2007 (consisting of seven books), and also writes the Junior Bender series (five books and counting) featuring an LA thief who also moonlights as a private eye. Hallinan has won the Lefty Award for best comic mystery for one of the Junior Bender books and his Poke Rafferty series gained attention from the judges of the Ian Fleming Steel Dagger. His books have also been nominated for the Edgar Awards, the Shamus Awards, the Macavity Awards and the Nero Awards. The usual screen options have been discussed, without (as yet) tangible results.

Why is it that some male readers will only read crime fiction by men? And, conversely, female readers are more attracted to such books by women? It's perhaps due to the fact that certain writers very specifically target their own constituency: Andy McNab, for instance, is well aware that his no-nonsense SAS thrillers are too testosterone-drenched for many women, while a whole army of female 'cosy' writers know that the gentility of their whodunits will alienate male readers. Actually, of course, the finest writers in the crime genre – both male and female – are read by both sexes, as they cannily avoid such pitfalls. Of American female crime writers, **DENISE HAMILTON** is a novelist whose readers are definitely not confined to one sex. Yes, she utilises a female protagonist – *LA Times* reporter Eve Diamond – but this index of female appeal is balanced by the hard-edged, masculine universe in which Eve moves.

This is a very modern version of Raymond Chandler's Los Angeles: sprawling, threatening and as threaded with corruption as it is with wealth. Several female crime writers pay lip service to Chandler, but Hamilton has done much more than that; she has thoroughly reinvented his milieu, reflecting the changes that have transformed the city since the 1930s. Eve Diamond is a pithily characterised heroine, prone to misjudgement but with a journalistic curiosity that is the perfect modern parallel for Philip Marlowe's dirt-digging. And the plots are quite as intriguingly labyrinthine as the master's – which makes it unsurprising that Hamilton's crime-writing cohorts are queuing up to praise her.

In *Savage Garden*, Eve is anticipating an evening at the theatre with her new man, Silvio Aguilar. But the famously unreliable leading lady, Catarina Velosi, is conspicuous by her absence – and Eve discovers that her new beau and the missing actress have a complicated (and mysterious) connection. When Silvio is blamed for the disappearance, Eve isn't buying it, but as she begins to dig into the actress's murky past, she encounters several very disparate characters: a libidinous political fixer, a theatre director who was one of Catarina's lovers, and his desperately jealous wife. And it's possible that one of them (or someone she hasn't met yet) will take the most drastic measures to ensure that she doesn't learn the truth. Readers will find that time spent in Eve's company is distinctly moreish.

North of Nowhere is a typically accomplished Alex McKnight novel from Edgar Award-winning **STEVE HAMILTON** and is set on the borders of Canada, vividly evoked here. The standards of Hamilton's earlier books are effortlessly maintained. Hamilton's hard-edged prose expertly encapsulates the violent contradictions in the lives of his characters. 'That summer, it was all about secrets… I already had one bullet inside me. I knew I didn't have room for another.' Alex McKnight rarely ventures out from his home these days, even to spend time at his friend Jackie's Glasgow Inn – he's had enough beatings. Even as he lets Jackie force him out one night for a poker game at a stranger's house, Alex is certain it's a bad idea. When the genial atmosphere rapidly deteriorates, he starts to think maybe he was right. And then three masked, armed robbers burst through the door, and things get a whole lot worse. Soon Alex's three closest friends are implicated in the robbery, and Alex becomes the object of hostile attention from the victim, not to mention a maniacal chihuahua. As events spin out of control, it becomes clear that somebody is not telling the truth and has put them all in terrible danger…

On a visit to the UK, Hamilton told me that he's happy to grab potential readers from Michael Connelly and James Lee Burke, but the author of *A Cold Day in Paradise*, *Winter of the Wolf Moon* and *The Hunting Wind* has his own fiefdom.

History can repeat itself. Just as **THOMAS HARRIS**'s novels *Red Dragon* and *The Silence of the Lambs* represented a double whammy that permanently reconfigured the crime fiction genre – and, as a subsequent by-product, the entire field of horror fiction – so the subsequent successful films of the books performed a concomitant shift in popular crime/horror cinema. *The Silence of the Lambs*, in particular, inaugurated a sea change in thriller cinema – the effects of which are being felt to this day, not least in the freighting in of extra layers of texture and resonance to narrative structure.

Many writers – whether in the crime or the horror field – envy Thomas Harris his unparalleled storytelling abilities. Harris has long since gone beyond being merely a top-flight writer: he is now a brand, and his sanguinary serial killer novels are the defining works of the genre. His name is routinely invoked – mostly in vain – for every new writer who attempts to cover the same territory. But there is only one Thomas Harris, and each novel (along with the film adaptations) featuring the super-intelligent aesthete and monster Hannibal Lecter is an event, nothing less. *Red Dragon* was the first book to introduce the cultivated serial killer, and its plot – including a unique symbiotic relationship between detective and prey – was very swiftly being imitated. *The Silence of the Lambs* took the phenomenon to a whole new level. Clarice Starling is a trainee FBI agent, working hard to discipline mind and body. She is sent by her boss, Section Chief Jack Crawford, to interview the serial killer Hannibal Lecter, kept in the very tightest security, to see if he's prepared to help in the case of a killer using a similar modus operandi. But the inexperienced Clarice is no match for the Machiavellian Lecter, and he begins to play highly sophisticated mind games with her, while the other monster – the non-incarcerated one – continues to ply his bloody trade. It's not hard to see why this remarkable book achieved such acclaim: it is, quite simply, a tour de force. And while Lecter may not be like any serial killer who ever walked the earth (most are dull, stupid men from a less privileged social class than Lecter, and most probably couldn't lecture on Italian Renaissance art), he remains the most iconic supercriminal in modern fiction. Given the phenomenal success of Thomas Harris's novel, the author could certainly have survived a maladroit cinema adaptation when the inevitable movie was made. In fact, the author was lucky: director Jonathan Demme got everything right, orchestrating the tension with the skill of a latter-day Alfred Hitchcock. The real success of the movie, however, lies in the casting of Jodie Foster, perfectly incarnating the out-of-her-depth Clarice, and Anthony Hopkins, masterly as the urbane Lecter – and even undercutting the Hollywood cliché of casting all well-spoken villains as Englishmen by utilising an impeccable American accent. Above all, the film (like the novel) is intelligent, a sharp contrast to most dumbed-down Hollywood fare.

The first outing for Thomas Harris's music- and art-loving psychopath, *Red Dragon*, is as comprehensively gripping as its successor. As well as the brilliantly delineated villain, there is a strong hero in Special Agent Will Graham, assigned to such cases as Lecter's because of his ability to intuitively place himself in the mind of monsters. As Harris had demonstrated in previous thrillers (such as *Black Sunday*, with its ever more relevant terrorist atrocity theme), his grasp of narrative structure is unswerving, and the careful, precision-timed parcelling out of plot information is one of the author's trademarks. But while others have attempted to imitate such tropes, none possess Harris's consummate mastery of characterisation – everybody in the novel is limned with painterly skill, whether in a few well-chosen lines or (like the monstrous Lecter) at satisfying length. Readers quickly realise that they can forget the million and one imitators who have followed: Thomas Harris is the *locus classicus* of the serial killer genre.

Red Dragon may have finally been filmed by Brett Ratner under its actual title (with Anthony Hopkins – now a shade too old for the role – tackling the part he has made his own for the last time), but the first screen incarnation of American serial killer Hannibal Lecter was by another British (and also Celtic) actor, Brian Cox, in Michael Mann's chillingly effective reading of the novel, renamed *Manhunter*. There are those who prefer Cox's more neutral, understated reading of the role, but such views often go hand in hand with a claim that whoever is extolling Cox's performance knew about the virtues of Mann's initially underrated movie before it became the *succès d'estime* it now is.

With the appearance of the Lecter 'prequel' *Hannibal Rising*, the knives were out for Thomas Harris – with quite as much deadly intent as his cultivated serial killer Hannibal Lecter ever harbours for his victims. After all, you can't be the world's bestselling thriller writer (along with the ubiquitous Dan Brown, whose books seem very sedate affairs alongside those of Harris) without people wanting you to fail – such is human nature. And this book – telling us about Lecter's early years and how he became the monster we know – is sufficiently different from what we expect from the author for it to draw hostile reactions from some critics, whatever the merits of the book might be.

Hannibal, the previous outing for Dr Lecter, had a controversial ending, with Clarice Starling forced into a drugged sexual relationship with her suave tormentor, and it was clear that the following book had to resolve that unpleasant cliffhanger. But that's precisely what *Hannibal Rising* doesn't do. We are taken back to Lecter's boyhood amid the bloodshed of World War Two. The young Hannibal watches his family slaughtered by the Nazis. But worse than this – and you should skip the rest of this paragraph if you dislike spoilers – something appalling happens to his beloved little sister at the hands of some truly unpleasant Nazi collaborators. The stage is set for massive, bloody revenge, as Hannibal tracks the men down.

Although the adult Lecter is in embryo here, the strategy of the book conforms to a pattern we expect from Harris. However unspeakable Hannibal's actions (and halfway through the book, there's an act of violence with a sword that will give the squeamish some nasty moments), he's usually up against individuals even worse than he is – such as his self-mutilated nemesis in the previous novel. Does this sleight of hand work? Can we enjoy Hannibal's gore-splattered revenge because it's not perpetrated against people like you or me, but against other monsters? That's up to the flexibility of the reader's own particular moral code. What critics of the book may pounce on is its relative straightforwardness, compared with the dense, fragmented novels that precede it. Everything here is subordinated to a linear tale of revenge, without the element that makes the other books so impressive: the contrast between his murderous protagonist and his vulnerable, conflicted, 'normal' opponents. The French copper here is a rudimentarily drawn figure, not given enough space to develop. Hannibal's motives and thought processes are not described beyond simple revenge. And the articulacy of the adult Lecter is sorely missed. But Harris is much too good a novelist not to ensure that this is a mesmerising read; everything, including the temporal sweep of the novel from wartime horrors to the civilised post-war Paris where Hannibal elects to live, is evoked with masterly skill. The sheer brio of the storytelling is irresistible, and then there's the flesh-shredding horror – nobody, but nobody, does that as chillingly as Thomas Harris. This will do to be going on with until the Hannibal story is finally resolved – and it sorely needs to be – in the next novel, if and when it appears.

Having served as a sheriff in north-eastern Iowa for 26 years, **DONALD HARSTAD** used his accumulated experience of the darker side of human nature to create the solidly written *Eleven Days*. And, pleasingly, *The Big Thaw* – the successor to *Eleven Days* and *The Known Dead* – proved to be equally impressive. In the later book, Nation County is suffering as the dead of winter exerts a paralysing grip. Deputy Sheriff Carl Houseman is dealing with the usual criminal fraternity of Iowa, while his partner and friend Hester Gorse has undertaken security duty on the floating casino *Colonel Beauregard*. Both will find themselves fighting for their lives when a ruthless group of men attempt a million-dollar siege of the economic assets of the state. Harstad's unerring tactics here involve a carefully orchestrated double jeopardy for his beleaguered protagonists: while Carl fights for control of the investigation and is at the extreme limit of his survival skills, Hester is trapped on the *Beauregard*, firmly in the eye of the storm. We've read the 'conflict between lawmen' scenario before, but rarely as adroitly handled as here – this is down to a combination of economical but rounded characterisation and a sense of verisimilitude that no doubt results from Harstad's long experience as a law officer. Hester, too, is a highly plausible creation – and her more direct experience of dangerous situations in the narrative means that she must carry the weight. The fact that Harstad pulls off this element of the plot as convincingly as Houseman's clashes with his fellow law enforcers is an index of his considerable skill.

My New Zealand friend and colleague Craig Sisterson (whose crime fiction expertise is unmatched) has said to me that he considers **JOHN HART** as a potential heir to James Lee Burke's title as greatest living American crime writer. Hart is the only author to win the Edgar Award for back-to-back novels, and he is also the recipient (for *The Last Child*) of the Crime Writers' Association's Ian Fleming Steel Dagger. In that book, teenager Johnny Merrimon has basked in the comfort of a good home and affectionate parents – not to mention a twin sister, Alyssa, to whom he is ineluctably bonded. The pain of loss hits Johnny with sledgehammer impact on the day that Alyssa disappears on a lonely street. A year passes, but he feels no sense of closure; no one else believes that Alyssa is still alive, but Johnny is convinced that she is, though for no logical reason. He decides to investigate the secrets, heretofore hidden, of his home town. And Detective Clyde Hunt has never stopped looking for Alyssa either. This is psychologically acute writing of a kind that is rare in the crime genre.

Iron House fulfilled expectations raised by Hart, and it's hardly surprising that no less a figure than Patricia Cornwell has been showering praise upon his striking writing. Two boys are left in an icy creek and forced to fight for their survival. Later, the younger of the two brothers kills his tormentor in a grim orphanage, while the older brother, Michael, assumes responsibility and runs to New York where he finds himself involved in organised crime. But after 20 years, he wants to leave the mob – something he will find extremely hard to do. *Down River* gleaned some of the best reviews of Hart's career, but other well-liked books include *The King of Lies*. Hart worked as a defence attorney and stockbroker, and writes his novels in North Carolina and Virginia.

Sometimes books arrive with such a prodigious word of mouth that they cannot possibly hope to match up to all the preliminary hype. And then there are books that prove to be quite as impressive as the bush telegraph has suggested – such a novel was **NOAH HAWLEY**'s

The Good Father. The jacket blurb evoked *We Need to Talk about Kevin*, but this is something different: confrontational in its treatment of the devastating effects of America's gun culture, but shot through with real emotional heft and featuring characters it is impossible not to care about.

Dr Paul Allen appears to be enjoying everything that society can offer: professional success and a contented family life resulting from his second marriage. But he is to see his cherished happiness lying in shreds when a crowd-pleasing presidential candidate is shot – and the gunman appears to be Paul's much-loved son. Daniel, the child of Paul's first marriage, has always been an unassuming boy, and his father is absolutely convinced that he is not capable of murder. A nightmare journey begins for the distressed parent, as Paul attempts to make sense of the series of catastrophic events that has destroyed his family – and he is to find, to his horror, that many of the most significant links between the events that led to the shooting had something to do with him and the decisions he made. The Lionel Shriver novel mentioned above is perhaps a fair comparison, but the central theme here – the extent of a parent's responsibility for a child's violent act – is beginning to appear in more novels, and is perhaps a sign of the nervousness about such issues on either side of the Atlantic. Noah Hawley has added to the debate with a novel that is, powerful, involving and full of provocative invective. As with all the best fiction, there are no cut-and-dried answers supplied here; Hawley is too intelligent a writer to force the reader into accepting any banal conclusions. We become ever more deeply involved with Paul Allen's attempts to find the truth behind the shooting – and to save the life of his son. America's National Rifle Association may take exception to the indictments on offer here, but the real theme is to what extent parents are responsible for their children's characters. Hawley suggests that Philip Larkin had it right in this area.

JULIA HEABERLIN told me that she was clinically dead before having her life saved by the fortuitous presence of a nurse in a restaurant when her heart stopped. Thankfully, she was spared – and the world of crime writing gained an unusual talent. Heaberlin's remarkable *Black-Eyed Susans* effortlessly rises above most of its competitors in terms of innovative, emotionally truthful writing. In this mesmerising novel, the haunted Tessa is the only survivor of a serial killer's reign of terror. But after several decades, she finds flowers planted outside her bedroom window. Is the murderous monster she escaped from still in prison – or closing in on her? In a crowded field, Heaberlin is something special, and clearly an author to whom close attention must be paid.

The tough world of the noir thriller is largely a male preserve; most of the key practitioners of the hard-boiled novel, from James M Cain to George Pelecanos, have been men, but there are women writers who have made some very successful forays into this unsettling territory. Near the peak of the distaff noir territory is **VICKI HENDRICKS** – and the lively Hendricks is not the kind of woman to be intimidated by the grimmer aspects of the genre, although she remains under-appreciated. In fact, her own lifestyle is probably a sight more punishing than the sedate existence of many of her male colleagues who tackle nothing more challenging than fitting a new ink cartridge into their printers. Her leisure pursuits (including romping with lions, skydiving, shark hunts and suchlike) render her machismo credentials impeccable, and *Sky Blues* is a copper-bottomed example of her no-punches-pulled, idiosyncratic prose. Hendricks' heroine Desi (short for Destiny) Donne is a woman who lives her life at the edge – rather like her creator. She is an exotic animal vet who is resolutely career-minded until she begins an affair with the charismatic Tom Jenks, who introduces her to the adrenalin rush that comes with the dangerous sport of skydiving. Her life becomes a heady cocktail of sex and danger, but then a savage murder complicates her whirl of sensual indulgence with Tom, and she finds herself faced with either a ruined life or an abruptly terminated one. This is splendid stuff: a heady narrative that exerts the kind of grip it is impossible to resist, while the prose has all the glittering sardonic nihilism that is the exclusive preserve of noir writing. The sexual passages have the unbuttoned steaminess that Hendricks has dished out before in such erotic thrillers as *Iguana Love* (this is not a book for the straitlaced). Best of all, Hendricks' heroine Desi is a totally plausible creation – even if we didn't know that the writer herself had such a nail-biting lifestyle, the verisimilitude of the plotting here fairly leaps off the page. If the idea appeals to you of stepping out of a small plane several thousand feet above the ground (and avoiding the temptation to pull the ripcord until you can smell the grass), *Sky Blues* is certainly the safest way to slake your lust for danger. It's also cheaper than charting a plane – and you live to tell the tale.

Apart from some nicely honed prose, the real enjoyment afforded the reader in *Murder in the Garden District* is **GREG HERREN**'s grasp of atmosphere and locale; both are delivered with real panache. The exterior of a beautiful Garden District mansion in New Orleans conceals the dark secrets of an influential family. A major hurricane is inexorably making its way towards the fearful city (already thoroughly devastated by Hurricane Katrina) and Herren's beleaguered protagonist Chanse MacLeod (a man who doesn't take no for an answer) has to winkle out the secrets behind a slew of murders and cover-ups before chaos and disorder reign once again.

It happens again and again. We pick up a new crime novel more in hope than expectation and our spirits drop when we realise we've been here before. Familiar plot, familiar characters... Do we really want to continue reading? But there is one writer who can always be guaranteed to make our jaws drop with his prodigality of invention. Take, for example, *Bad Monkey*, a typical **CARL HIAASEN** Catherine wheel, showering out sprays of comically outlandish plotting and effects. Over the top? Perhaps.

Miami policeman-turned-restaurant inspector Andrew Yancy's career is on a downward spiral, not helped by his assaults on the husband of his girlfriend. He sees, however, a chance of redemption in the unlikely form of a severed human arm, chewed off by a shark. He attempts to reconnect it (metaphorically speaking) to the body to which it once belonged, and undertakes a memorably grotesque odyssey that has all the accoutrements of a rundown amusement park. Yancy runs into – and raucously intersects with – a truly bizarre cast of characters, notably the owner of the severed arm, an ex-inamorata of his own who won't let go, a coroner with unusual sexual tastes and a toothless Bahamian voodoo priestess. (Not to mention the bloody-minded simian of the title.) And if the dramatis personae listed here doesn't convey the full panoply of what is on offer, one might add the fatal consequences of Yancy's interviews with several of the above, along with encounters with his own hapless doppelgänger. Not enough? There's a hurricane, house burnings and frequent outbursts of over-the-top violence. Other writers may attempt to emulate Hiaasen's crowded plots, but it's not just the latter that need to be replicated but the very individual, sardonic tone of voice that at times is suggestive of an American version of the late Tom Sharpe (with added mayhem).

Of course, there are those who prefer more grounded, realistic fare than that to be found in a novel such as this, with characters who move in something like the same world as the rest of us – and who is to gainsay such preferences? But for those prepared to strap themselves in for the roller coaster ride that is a Carl Hiaasen novel – those, in other words, for whom 'excess' is not a dirty word – *Bad Monkey* can be guaranteed to pleasurably shake the fillings loose from the teeth.

As one of the most inventive and entertaining of modern crime writers, Hiaasen's influence on the genre has been so all-encompassing that his punchy, brittle-edged prose and sardonic humour may be found reproduced in the work of a hundred imitators. There is no doubt that Hiaasen is at the top of the tree in his chosen field – so why did he suddenly choose to produce his first novel for young readers? And many readers of the author will be asking another question: is the book equally entertaining for the older reader as it is for its target audience? The answer to the latter is certainly yes, although a certain scaling down of adult expectations might be in order. The youthful protagonist of *Hoot*, Roy Eberhardt, is not enjoying his family's move to the sprawling, sultry state of Florida. Roy is learning to deal with aggressive kids at school (such as the intimidating Dana Mathereson), when a curious incident happens: he sees a boy while on the way to school who piques his interest. A shoeless boy is running from the school bus, and when Roy tracks him down, he encounters mysteries connected with his disturbed new friend that drag him out of his precarious new life into a world of danger. And one of the most pressing problems he becomes involved in is a pending threat to Florida wildlife – an issue that Roy can do something about, provided he's prepared to risk behaving in an illegal fashion. While Florida in this novel is not quite the manic and surrealistic place it is in the author's adult books, it's still drawn with great quirkiness and imagination. Younger readers looking for something a little more substantial than most teenage fare would be well advised to pick this one up.

NAOMI HIRAHARA is the celebrated Asian-American creator of the Mas Arai series (the protagonist is an ageing Japanese-American gardener-cum-detective), among other books. Hirahara bagged an Edgar Award for *Snakeskin Shamishen* in 2007, and while largely unknown outside the US, the author has enjoyed both critical and commercial acclaim, her books featuring in various 'Top Ten Mysteries of the Year' lists.

Thomas Harris and *The Silence of the Lambs* provided the prototype for **TAMI HOAG**'s spellbinder *Ashes to Ashes*, in which FBI agent Kate Conlan and her former lover hunt the Cremator, a serial killer with the grim modus operandi of burning his female victims alive. *Ashes to Ashes* is not a book for the squeamish, and neither is the equally impressive *Dust to Dust*. But, as before, grisly tension is not the only commodity on offer here – the internal politics of the police investigations are handled with genuine panache, and Hoag's protagonist Sam Kovac and his partner Nikki Liska are very solidly drawn.

When internal affairs investigator Andy Fallon appears to take his own life, a metaphorical time bomb is set under the Minneapolis Police Department. Fallon (who was gay) was looking into a possible police connection in the death of another gay officer. The laconic Kovac finds a labyrinth of deception and intrigue when he begins his investigation, and – as is par for the course for all police thrillers – heavy pressure is soon coming down from on high to terminate the case. Hoag has demonstrated in such intelligent novels as *A Thin Dark Line* and *Guilty as Sin* an effortless command of thriller technique, adroitly juggling the twin demands of character and plot. This is a cooler and more restrained book than its predecessor, but no less dynamic for all that. The set-piece confrontations will ensure that it will take quite a lot to distract the reader from Hoag's narrative, and the use of short, idiosyncratic paragraphs in the closing chapters is an innovative touch.

If you're tired of Home Counties crime penned by genteel ladies, and your taste is for redder meat by female American writers, you will no doubt already have Kathy Reichs, Karin Slaughter and Patricia Cornwell on your reading list. And now there's another name to add to that list: **JILLIANE HOFFMAN**. Hoffman's *Retribution* established the writer as one of the most uncompromising practitioners in the serial killer field, and *Last Witness* consolidated the sterling work done in that book. A savage serial killer known as Cupid cut a bloody swathe through Miami two years before the narrative of *Last Witness*, torturing and murdering 11 young women. In the present, fear stalks Miami Beach once again, when three police officers are killed and gruesomely mutilated while on patrol. What's the linking factor? All three of the dead cops had been involved in the Cupid investigation. This is worrying news for Assistant State Attorney CJ Townsend, who also worked on the Cupid case. She is party to a secret shared by the dead officers, and it's hardly rocket science to deduce that her name is almost certainly next on the bloodstained list. As in *Retribution*, all of this is dispatched with maximum efficiency by the unsentimental Hoffman. While the character of the attorney heroine perhaps doesn't add any new wrinkles to the genre, Hoffman is savvy enough a writer to ring the changes and render her a winning and sympathetic protagonist.

Like so many writers, **CHRIS HOLM** was first published in such titles as *Ellery Queen's Mystery Magazine* and *Alfred Hitchcock's Mystery Magazine*. He has been nominated for a number of awards, including three Anthonys, two Derringers, two Spinetinglers, a Barry, a Lefty, and a Macavity – and he's managed to win several. Holm's The Collector trilogy relocates the conflict between heaven and hell into traditional pulp crime territory. Other work includes his Michael Hendricks novels (notably *The Killing Kind*) with a protagonist whose targets are fellow hitmen.

There is a certain laziness in the world of books – among those who publish them and those who sell them. It's the comparisons to other authors on the jacket; perhaps we readers are lazy too – after all, the shorthand is for us. And if you're a lawyer-turned-novelist, you can expect to see John Grisham's name hopefully invoked in your publicity. A recent candidate for this treatment is **DAVID HOSP**, with his novel *Among Thieves*. But the Grisham namecheck doesn't actually do Hosp any favours – as anyone who reads the novel will see.

Hosp has been around for some time; in his debut novel, *Dark Harbour*, he exposed the workings of a group of merciless terrorists, and terrorists are back in this novel. Hosp's lawyer hero, Scott Finn, is markedly more individual than the wearying army of such protagonists from Grisham wannabes – and Hosp himself (a trial lawyer who writes his books on a daily commute by boat across Boston harbour) is clearly in possession of more solid storytelling skills than most Grishamites. What's more – and this is what makes the Grisham comparison a little ironic – he's actually a better writer than his predecessor.

Defence attorney Scott Finn takes on a criminal, Devon Malley, as a client – the fact that he is obviously guilty is par for the course. But a more ill-advised move for Finn is to agree to take on responsibility for Malley's daughter Sally. Malley has a persuasive reason for being in jail: art stolen in a major robbery has yet to be recovered, and there is a ruthless individual from the past with violent revenge in mind. And Scott Finn finds himself in the firing line.

While *Among Thieves* moves like an express train, the real pleasure comes from character interaction, notably Scott's ham-fisted attempts to relate to the difficult Sally. And in an ambitious plot that involves the Troubles and ruthless members of the IRA, extreme violence is the order of the day (Hosp pulls no punches here). The Boston setting is a reminder of another novelist, Dennis Lehane, the great chronicler of the city. In fact, Hosp's achievement is closer to that of his fellow Bostonian than to the more straightforward narratives of John Grisham. Perhaps we don't need any more lawyers making the career switch to novelist, but readers can be thankful that David Hosp took this particular route. .

STEPHEN HUNTER, originally from Kansas City, Missouri, made a mark with such novels as *Point of Impact* (filmed as *Shooter*), *Black Light* and *Time to Hunt*, which form an initial trilogy featuring Bob 'the Nailer' Swagger. More Swagger outings followed after a gap of almost ten years, including *Night of Thunder* and *Dead Zero*. As well as other novels, Hunter has also written non-fiction, such as *Violent Screen: A Critic's 13 Years on the Front Lines of Movie Mayhem*, essays culled from his newspaper work, and is well known for his defence of US gun ownership.

With a multiplicity of elements to praise, it's hard to know where to start first with such **GREGG HURWITZ** novels as *Tell No Lies* (with its beleaguered probation counsellor Daniel Brasher knee deep in a series of gruesome murders). The book exerts all the author's customary Ancient Mariner-like grip on the reader, and is sometimes reminiscent of another American master, Harlan Coben, but Hurwitz is always fully aware of the importance of character kept firmly at the centre of the helter-skelter plotting. And it's not just crime novels; the author has brought new levels of sophistication to his much acclaimed run on *Batman* (having, for instance, Bruce Wayne appreciate Ravel's piano masterpiece *Gaspard de la Nuit*). All of this demonstrates a welcome readiness not to be pigeonholed, although, perhaps, his comics work is not such a stretch – after all, the Dark Knight took over from Sherlock Holmes the soubriquet of the World's Greatest Detective. Film options also beckon for Hurwitz.

Los Angeles resident **CHARLIE HUSTON** divides his energies between novels and TV. One project was *Powers*, a drama series based on the comic book created by Brian Michael Bendis and Michael Avon Oeming. Huston's books include *Skinner*, *Sleepless* and *The Shotgun Rule*, along with the Henry Thompson trilogy and the Joe Pitt Casebooks, not to mention several titles for Marvel Comics. His TV projects have included an HBO pilot based on his *The Mystic Arts of Erasing All Signs of Death*, executive produced and directed by *True Blood* creator Alan Ball.

When visiting the UK, the saturnine **GREG ILES**, the author of the epic *Natchez Burning*, is wont to wrong-foot the British with his laid-back, self-described 'good ole boy' persona. 'But I really am a good ole boy,' he once argued to a sceptical group I was with. Iles maintained to his British listeners that he was a typical Southerner: gun-owning, possum-shooting ('Hell, my brother even voted for George W!'). No one was deceived, however, as the laser-sharp wit behind the Southern drawl – and the use of such adjectives as 'egregiously' – somewhat undercut the 'jes' plain folks' image. Iles' tales of fighting Charlize Theron over sex scenes in a film of one of his books (she wanted to take her shirt off, he didn't want her to) had his listeners entranced, if disbelieving. *Natchez Burning* is typical Iles fare: colourful, pungent, and brimming with lashings of atmosphere. His work deserves greater acknowledgment on non-US shores.

The Mulholland books imprint in the UK may not have created quite the stir that its parent company Hodder and Stoughton hoped for, but for the real cognoscenti of the crime fiction genre, the name of the imprint has long been a guarantee of some of the most individual and cogent writing in the field, with **LISA JACKSON** one of the stars of the Mulholland crown, as the highly readable *Cold Blooded* proves on page after page. A woman's slashed, incinerated corpse is found in a seedy New Orleans apartment. From her bed in a bayou cottage on the outskirts of town, Olivia Bechet has a vision of the murder. In *Lost Souls*, three girls have disappeared at All Saints College. The police are not interested, but Kristi Bentz, who has survived the attack of a serial killer, begins to investigate the lives of the missing girls. There is an unusual combination on offer here: strong, economical characterisation, a vivid sense of place and a grasp of storytelling that marks Lisa Jackson out from the crowd. *Lost Souls* incorporates fresh elements into a highly compulsive read.

RYAN DAVID JAHN published his much-acclaimed first novel, *Acts of Violence*, which went on to win the Crime Writers' Association's (CWA's) John Creasey Dagger, in 2009, and has since published other books that have enjoyed success: *Low Life*, *The Dispatcher* (long-listed for the CWA's Ian Fleming Steel Dagger), *The Last Tomorrow*, *The Gentle Assassin* and *Dark Hours*.

JA JANCE has written more than 50 books since her mid-1980s debut, including three acclaimed – and lengthy – series of books featuring retired Seattle Police Department Detective JP Beaumont, Arizona County Sheriff Joanna Brady, and former Los Angeles news anchor-turned-sleuth Ali Reynolds. She has been nominated for an Anthony Award on several occasions as well as for a Dilys Award. She splits her time between Seattle and Arizona.

When a publisher splashes a rave by a celebrated writer across a book's jacket to sell a new author, there is a twofold purpose: firstly to inform us that somebody we probably enjoy reading thinks the book is a winner; and secondly to hint that this writer shares some of the qualities of the better-known author who is raving about them. So when **IRIS JOHANSEN**'s *Body of Lies* bore the legend 'Iris Johansen is incomparable' by no less than Tami Hoag, we could be forgiven for thinking that she is a writer in a similar vein: razor-sharp plotting and a particular emphasis on the psychology of the characters. Readers can decide for themselves. Johansen's heroine Eve Duncan (yet another – sigh – forensics expert, though here a 'forensics sculptor') is drawn with intelligence and sympathy and is a protagonist who has possibilities of longevity in the genre. Eve finds herself landed with a high-security job, dropped in her lap by a top government official. The corpse of a murder victim is to be her subject, but stringent security means that she has been given virtually no background information. And as a reconstruction begins, she realises that there is a highly intelligent killer at work who will stop at nothing to ensure Eve's investigations come to an end. There is, of course, a malign conspiracy at the heart of this thriller, and Eve Duncan's steady unpeeling of the various layers of plot is handled with assurance and skill.

CRAIG JOHNSON's Sheriff Walt Longmire novels include *The Cold Dish* (the inaugural book in the series) and *The Dark Horse* (which was named one of *Publishers Weekly*'s best books of the year in 2009). A successful TV series, *Longmire*, was adapted from Johnson's novels and premiered in 2012. Johnson's fame has even generated an annual festival, called Longmire Days, in Buffalo, Wyoming. The author, many of the actors, and (on occasion) the publishers and producers attend this large-scale event.

It was the crime novelist David Baldacci who supplied an encomium for **MARSHALL KARP**'s debut, but perhaps Carl Hiaasen should have been approached, as the frenetic plotting and outrageous characterisation are more in his line than Baldacci's. In *The Rabbit Factory*, the rabbit mascot of a studio theme park, Familyland, is killed, and the park's executives want to keep a lid on things. It's down to LAPD detectives Mike Lomax and Terry Biggs to crack a case that's becoming ever more bloody – and it's clear that someone may have a very large grudge against the studio. Hiaasen is certainly one of the prototypes for this outing, but the anti-establishment humour (not to mention the arm-straining length of the book) is reminiscent of another darkly humorous novelist, Joseph Heller. Lomax and Biggs were promising protagonists, and although this first outing hardly made a sales breakthrough, the series is still ongoing. Karp also writes the NYPD Red series with James Patterson.

ALEX KAVA is the creator of the much-liked Maggie O'Dell series and a later sequence featuring former marine Ryder Creed. Her standalone novel, *One False Move*, was followed by the political thriller, *Whitewash*. She is also a co-author of the novellas *Slices of Night* and *Storm Season* with Erica Spindler and JT Ellison and is a founding member of International Thriller Writers.

The following three entries address a crime-writing dynasty – one that proves that nepotism does not mean that the family members need be mere recipients of largesse blessed only with slender talents. In fact, when I met the scion of the Kellerman family, the youthful Jesse, he politely suggested I may have arrived with preconceptions – and not good ones. But, approaching them alphabetically by first name, let's first address **FAYE KELLERMAN**. Her *Blindman's Bluff* is a typically persuasive title from the distaff side of the Kellerman family, and Faye's page-turning narrative is one of her best. When a wealthy man and his family are murdered on their impressive estate (despite extensive – and expensive – security), it's up to Lieutenant

Peter Decker of the LAPD to find out what happened. The trouble is that the dead man's massive business empire throws up a wealth of suspects: business partners, members of security, other captains of industry and even members of his own family. Kellerman is on cracking form, delivering her narrative with the customary assurance.

Back to nepotism... or perhaps not? Did the debut novel by **JESSE KELLERMAN**, the son of acclaimed thriller writers Jonathan and Faye Kellerman, have anything to offer in its own right? In *Sunstroke*, Gloria Mendez is fixated upon her boss Carl. And then Carl vanishes, and when his body turns up in a town in Mexico, his murder has a catastrophic effect on Gloria. In a fractured emotional state, she wanders around Mexico, trying to find out what was behind his death. Unsurprisingly, she uncovers some very unsavoury secrets. So is Kellerman *fils* a chip off two old blocks? The answer is not a simple one: certainly this is an adroitly written thriller, and the obsessed Gloria is a strongly characterised protagonist. But would the book have seen the light of day if the manuscript had landed on an editorial desk without the Kellerman family moniker? As Jesse said to me, family association might provide you with an entrée, but continued success depends on individual achievement – hanging on to mom and pop's coat-tails won't keep your career in motion.

Finally in this trio, let's look at the paterfamilias, **JONATHAN KELLERMAN**. The author's Alex Delaware thrillers have amassed a devoted following, and the reasons for this are readily apparent. In such books as *When the Bough Breaks* and *Over the Edge*, Kellerman utilised his background as a paediatric psychologist to create a profession for his hero (who is a crack practitioner) of total verisimilitude. In the first books, Alex, though officially retired, took on cases referred to him by Milo Sturgis of the LAPD, and a recurrent theme was that of damaged children suffering from emotional or physical abandonment by parents – and that is (to some degree) the theme of *Flesh and Blood*. When Alex Delaware first sees Lauren, she is a teenager with all the usual problems – moody, uncommunicative, resentful of her parents. But years later, at a bachelor party, Alex is watching two strippers go through a graphic display – and one of them is the unhappy Lauren. Then she disappears – and we're off into familiar Delaware thriller territory, delivered with all the aplomb we expect from the reliable Kellerman. In earlier books, Alex was occasionally portrayed as being a little too prescient, but Kellerman has given his hero a satisfyingly conflicted emotional life, and his personal involvement here gives *Flesh and Blood* a strong underpinning of drama that counterpoints the central mystery and sharpens it at every point. Only Kellerman's earlier *Billy Straight* displayed the same degree of penetrating psychological insight and an unvarnished view of human nature – here, the plotting is even more assured and trenchant. In the Kellerman family, he is – in every sense – the Daddy.

It's becoming more and more tricky to import fresh elements into the increasingly shop-worn serial killer genre, but **JACK KERLEY** pulls off the trick with *The Hundredth Man*, a keenly honed thriller that even manages to transform a key cliché of the genre: the detective struggling with his own demons while tracking down a relentless murderer. Kerley is an author who deserves the five-star treatment his publisher gave him on this book, and there is much here to commend: the author is highly persuasive with both his sultry Alabama setting and the labyrinthine machinations of police department politics. His troubled protagonist, Carson Ryder, is less convinced than his colleagues that the decapitated body found in his district is that of a male prostitute. And Ryder has a dark secret in his own past – and finding out the truth behind a new series of killings will involve great personal danger, physical and moral.

KAREN KIJEWSKI was born in Berkeley, California, and her quirky books featuring private eye Kat Colorado include *Katapult*, *Copy Kat* and *Stray Kat Waltz*. Her first book, *Katwalk*, while not enjoying universal acclaim, bagged the 1990 Anthony Award and the Shamus Award that year, both for best first novel.

As many readers are less patient these days with books that don't grab the attention within a few chapters, the writer has to work considerably harder than in the past. With *The Blue Edge of Midnight*,

JONATHON KING demonstrated with some skill that he knew the rules of the game, and quickly established himself as an interesting new talent. From the fetid edges of the Everglades to the dangerous corners of Philadelphia, King strip-mines the thriller genre to come up with something fresh and arresting. Max Freeman's life changed forever one night when he killed a 12-year-old child in self-defence in a Philadelphia shoot-out. That was the end of his career in the police, and now he lives a solitary existence on the edge of the Florida Everglades, struggling with the nagging voices of his conscience. And then he encounters the body of a child near an ancient river; soon, he finds himself at the centre of the search for a serial killer, and past and present grimly collide. Distrusted by both the residents of the Glades and the police (who regard him as a suspect), Max ponders what to do – and then another child goes missing and Max decides that he must hunt down the murderer himself. Perhaps we've encountered this plot before, but it's harder and harder to find fresh narrative devices when everything has been recycled so often. Notwithstanding this caveat, *The Blue Edge of Midnight* is strongly written stuff; a thriller that never lets go.

When you are one of the world's most successful authors, it can be a risky business switching from the genre in which you are best known. Some years ago, the crime writer James Patterson felt the desire to get out of his system a series of saccharine romantic novels that did not excite the fans of his thrillers. It is, however, a different matter for **STEPHEN KING**, who has long been the undisputed monarch of the horror thriller but who has a deep personal love for the crime genre.

Mr Mercedes, while not his first venture into the crime field, is (so far) his best. It is a tense, ticking-clock thriller that sets a burned-out cop against a demented mass murderer who is planning an act of carnage to match the one with which he started his criminal career. The opening of the novel is a tour de force, the kind of curtain-raiser that King admirers relish. In a Midwestern city, crowds of unemployed, desperate people wait in frigid temperatures for the slim chance that they will be hired at a job fair. We meet two people in the queue, a down-on-his-luck young man and a mother who has been forced to bring her baby, who is coughing in the cold. Their characters are described with such vividness and warmth that we are in no doubt that these will be the protagonists of the book. But then a Mercedes suddenly appears – which subsequently proves to have been stolen – and with shocking suddenness, the driver ploughs the car into the crowd, reverses, and drives over his victims again. Eight people are killed and 15 wounded, among them the characters who we have assumed we will be following throughout the book. The car is abandoned and the killer escapes, leaving no trace.

A year passes and retired policeman Bill Hodges receives a deeply disturbing letter from a mysterious individual who lays claim to being the perpetrator of the act of random murder, and who tells Hodges that he is in the early stages of planning an even more gruesome attack. Hodges, still suffering from guilt from being unable to crack the earlier case, is drawn out of his unhappy retirement to engage in a battle of wits worthy of Holmes and Moriarty – or Hannibal Lecter and Clarice Starling.

Those who might be reluctant to follow Stephen King into an unfamiliar genre should not hesitate; all of the narrative skill that distinguishes his fantasy work is firmly in place here, including those shocking hints of what is to follow ('One of the young men... had been staring at Janice Cray – this was Keith Frias, whose left arm would shortly be torn from his body'), and the familiar orchestration of mounting tension shows the author's usual command. And if the basic scenario is a familiar one, the characterisation is faultless. There is the depressive detective hero with an ever-present gun on his table, toying with the idea of suicide; similarly memorable is the terrifying psychopathic killer (with perhaps a little of the DNA of motel proprietor Norman Bates), living with his alcoholic mother in a house filled with secrets. Admittedly, we are reminded that crime fiction is not King's default territory: a lengthy description of the horrors of daytime reality TV shows (which the suicidal Hodges glumly watches) outstays its welcome, and both hero and villain are cut from a very familiar cloth. But King aficionados will be riveted from the first explosion of violence to the final, equally seismic, climax. The writer's fans won't be complaining when he turns to crime again – as he is doing.

ANDREW KLAVAN has long been one of the most tough and uncompromising of American crime writers, with a particular interest in social issues. His concern, for instance, with themes of child abuse resulted in some trenchant novels long before the concept was taken up by other writers – and before it became such a key concern of modern society. Such books as *Damnation Street* are more conventional but are still handled with the assurance that we expect from Klavan. Private eye Scott Weiss works in San Francisco, and shares with Raymond Chandler's Philip Marlowe a dogged devotion to the job along with a certain inappropriate but romantic knight errantry. He is being tracked down by a deeply unpleasant hitman called the Shadowman, and he strikes up a friendship with another denizen of the hotel where he is staying: the attractive, but deeply screwed-up, Jim, whose taste for drugs and dangerous women has got him into trouble in the past. In an echo of Patricia Highsmith's *Strangers on a Train*, the two men swap problems, with Jim deciding to track down the Shadowman before he can nail Scott. There's absolutely nothing wrong with using a familiar theme, particularly when novel changes can be rung on it – and that's precisely what Andrew Klavan does here. Written in similarly professional fashion is *The Identity Man*, which features John Shannon as a petty criminal who has been framed for murder. A nationwide manhunt is under way for him, but Shannon believes that he is off the radar. But then a strange text message summons him to a meeting at night. A nameless foreigner who identifies himself as 'The Identity Man' appears to offer Shannon everything he needs: new papers, a new life in a city that has suffered from floods – even a new face. For Shannon, it is a chance to begin again, and soon he meets a beguiling woman. But, needless to say, his troubles are by no means over.

The prolific **DEAN KOONTZ** is something of an institution – perhaps an over-familiar one – bestselling and efficient, but not necessarily innovative. His fans were pleased with such books as *From the Corner of his Eye* and *One Door Away from Heaven*, even if critics paid little attention. *By the Light of the Moon* is typical Koontz. Artist Dylan O'Connor is driving through Arizona with his autistic brother

Shepherd, à la *Rain Man*, and decides to catch up on his sleep in a motel. But (as Hitchcock and Robert Bloch demonstrated) motels can be dangerous places, and he is soon tied up, gagged and being pumped full of strange fluid by a sinister doctor. At the same time, comedian Jillian Jackson is watching her career feebly playing out in a succession of downmarket comedy joints. All her dreams of changing her life are torpedoed when she, too, becomes a victim of the deranged scientist, who steals her car. Then begins a lunatic chase, involving the doctor and his victims, and the surfaces of reality quickly become very insubstantial. As the above demonstrates, this novel is quite different from earlier books by the author – and, it has to be said, unlike work by fellow thriller writers. It may, counterintuitively, be the best book for the Koontz novice to sample.

Over the course of several novels, **MICHAEL KORYTA** has established himself as an extremely skilful thriller writer, with a particularly impressive list of fellow writers lining up to grant encomiums; these include Michael Connelly, Dennis Lehane and Stephen King – although the latter, of course, is especially generous in his granting of such largesse. Koryta's novel *Envy the Night* won the *Los Angeles Times* Book Prize, and the writer has put to fruitful use his own background as a former private investigator and newspaper reporter. *The Prophet* is a particularly strong and inventive thriller that exerts a relentless grip on the reader. Because of an event in the past, the lives of two brothers have been changed irrevocably. As a teenager, a decision made by Adam Austin led to the death of his sister. His brother Kent has found a way to be charitable to the girl's murderer, but he has never completely forgiven his brother. Twenty years pass, and the two men's lives have taken very different routes, but when Adam agrees to assist a young woman in tracking down her missing father, she is murdered – and Adam is reminded of the events that changed his life. When it becomes necessary to deal with the past, the two men are to have strikingly different approaches – and the decisions they make will be fateful.

Plotting is, of course, always crucial in thrillers such as *The Prophet*, but the real skill here lies in the diamond-sharp characterisation – it is precisely because we care about the characters that we find ourselves so involved. The novel is another winner for Michael Koryta.

WILLIAM KENT KRUEGER was born in Torrington, Wyoming, and led a peripatetic life as a child in a variety of different houses and different cities. Passionately inspired by the writer Ernest Hemingway, Krueger's own books include a mystery series set in the north woods of Minnesota. His central character is Cork O'Connor, ex-sheriff of Tamarack County and a man of complicated ethnicity: part Irish and part Ojibwe. The O'Connor sequence has won the Anthony Award three times – including back to back in 2005 and 2006 – and also the Barry Award, among others. By 2016, Krueger had published 16 books, some of which are standalones; he won the Edgar Award for best novel in 2013 for his standalone *Ordinary Grace*.

JON LAND's books include the Caitlin Strong sequence featuring a fifth-generation Texas ranger, and a separate series featuring Ben Kamal and Danielle Barnea, a Palestinian detective and a chief inspector in the Israeli police. He is an emeritus board member of the International Thriller Writers, and worked on the screenplay for the film *Dirty Deeds*.

Parents sometimes worry about a lack of communication with their children, but they tend to convince themselves that monosyllabic, difficult teenagers are the norm – and that is precisely what Andy Barber (a prosecutor in Massachusetts) and his wife Laurie assume with regard to the tricky relationship with their son, Jacob. But then one of Jacob's classmates is discovered dead in a nearby park. Andy is summoned to the murder scene by the police and his suspicions fall on a paedophile who lives in the area. But then it is revealed that Andy's son discovered the body, had a knife in his possession – and had a motive for the killing. The odds stacked against Andy and his son are ratcheted up by a rival in the prosecutor's office who takes over the murder case and decides that there is enough evidence to secure a conviction.

In all the best legal thrillers – and **WILLIAM LANDAY**'s *Defending Jacob* is one of the best – it is crucial that we worry about the insuperable problems loaded on the shoulders of the central characters, and Landay handles that aspect with authority. Andy's wife, Laurie, is a vulnerable individual who quickly begins to buckle under the tension affecting the family, and Jacob does himself no favours by posting what he describes as jokey messages on Facebook in which he appears to implicate himself. Under most pressure is Andy, who sees his career as a prosecutor slipping away from him – and so even if he is able to save his son, destitution beckons. Could things get worse? Yes they could – there is a dark secret in Andy's past: three generations on the male side of his family have been murderers… is this a genetic inevitability?

Word of mouth on a new novel is not always to be trusted, but sometimes a book handsomely fulfils all the expectations – such a novel was *Defending Jacob*. Like Scott Turow, Landay is a lawyer who made his mark as a prosecutor before literary success beckoned. If Turow's *Presumed Innocent* remains the definitive legal thriller, *Defending Jacob* is one of the most accomplished entries among the army of similar books that have followed in its wake.

Among writers in what is loosely called the crime and thriller genre, **JOE R LANSDALE** is an absolutely unique talent. In fact, his sardonically funny, atmospherically realised novels barely fit in any recognised genre, although violent death can be counted on as a recurring factor. Such books as *Bad Chili* and *Captains Outrageous* have carved out a Lansdalian universe, unlike that of any other writer (apart, of course, from his growing host of imitators). Set in the 1930s, *Sunset and Sawdust* was something of a departure. Sunset is the widow of the local constable, whom she shot dead in self-defence at a Texan sawmill camp. However, her assumption of her husband's role, as she undertakes an investigation into a double murder, is looked at askance by the uncooperative townsfolk – and some bizarre encounters are in store for the gun-toting Sunset. Over-the-top characters, delirious plotting, a vividly drawn milieu, and coruscating dialogue: all the customary Joe Lansdale fingerprints are in place. Lansdale, always entertaining company, told me how he'd mischievously enjoyed instilling excessive violence into a proscribed area – not one of his own novels, but when writing for the *Batman* animated TV series. He found that he could inflict massive physical destruction – but only on a ventriloquist's dummy.

ALICE LAPLANTE is the winner of the Wellcome Trust Book Prize, and proves in her economical but compelling novel *Turn of Mind* that she is a storyteller of genuine acumen. The central character is a woman who is in the process of losing her mind. Jennifer White was once a renowned surgeon, but when her best friend Amanda is found murdered, there is a macabre detail: four of the dead woman's fingers have been removed, clearly by an expert. Inevitably, suspicion of responsibility for the killing has fallen upon her. *Turn of Mind* is an absolute winner.

Phenomenal word of mouth regarding a new novel is not always justified, but it assuredly was in the case of **VICTOR LAVALLE**'s *Big Machine*, a truly phantasmagorical experience that is quite unlike anything you will have encountered before. Comparisons have been made with Gabriel García Márquez and Edgar Allan Poe, which perhaps gives some indication of the territory covered here, but it's the merest indication of the bizarre and immersive experience of the book. The anti-hero of LaValle's novel is middle-aged junkie Ricky Rice, who has survived a terminal involvement in a suicide cult and now ekes out an existence working as a porter in a New York bus depot. He receives a letter reminding him that he made a grim vow in his past, and ordering him to travel to a remote part of Vermont to discharge his obligation. But on arrival, Ricky finds himself involved with a group of paranormal investigators – ex-addicts and criminals like himself, all of whom have heard 'The Voice', which may or may not (they consider) be God speaking to them. At the end of a bizarre, sometimes hilarious and often nightmarish journey, Ricky is confronted with the extremes of belief and madness.

Apart from the sheer exhilaration produced by this nicely ill-mannered narrative, the off-kilter pleasures afforded by *Big Machine* include both a truly dark and sardonic vision of the world and a lacerating analysis of the sinister side of faith and belief. LaValle is very much a writer to watch.

OWEN LAUKKANEN's 2012 debut *The Professionals* gleaned enthusiastic reviews. The narrative involved four recent university graduates who turn to kidnapping in a failing job market. The book gained praise from John Sandford and CJ Box. Laukkanen followed this up with the accomplished *Criminal Enterprise*, reuniting FBI Special Agent Carla Windermere and Minnesota state investigator Kirk Stevens.

When crime readers concur on the merits of a certain author, that's a reason to pay attention. But when similar acclaim comes from fellow practitioners, readers really need to mark their cards. The great **DENNIS LEHANE** has become a must-read novelist on the strength of such gritty and forceful thrillers as *Darkness, Take My Hand* and *Gone, Baby, Gone*. Praised for his taut, carefully orchestrated storylines and expressively drawn, vulnerable characters, Lehane is the kind of writer who has achieved his position by stealth rather than massive advertising campaigns. *Mystic River* confirmed his status as one of the most vigorous and skilful American talents in years. Childhood friends, Sean, Jimmy and Dave have their lives changed when a strange car turns up in their street. After one boy gets into the car while the other two don't, a terrible event happens that terminates their friendship and changes their lives. Twenty-five years later, Sean is a homicide detective, while Jimmy has taken a criminal route. When Jimmy's daughter is found savagely killed, Sean is assigned to the case. And with his own personal relationships in deep trouble, he finds he is obliged to go back to the life he thought he had left behind, coming to terms with his ex-friends and a confrontation with a human monster. As psychological thrillers go, this one is dispatched with authority.

Live By Night is another accomplished Dennis Lehane novel, one that posed a question: what should a writer do when they have painted themselves into a corner? Literary success in one genre can be a straitjacket, but readers don't necessarily have the patience to indulge their favourites when they strike out into new territory. However, such changes of direction are not an issue for Dennis Lehane, who has long taken a far more organic approach to the trajectory of his work – his books have blossomed from straightforward thrillers into something more complex: crime epics with an impressive historical sweep.

Lehane's *The Given Day* weighed in at over 700 pages, but its successor, *Live By Night* – while leaner and more focused – still has a daunting reach, with a background of the Prohibition era and the vicious gangsters who flourished at the time. The timespan of the novel is a decade, beginning in 1920s Boston and moving to Tampa and Cuba as we follow the tribulations of Joe Coughlin. Despite his respectable antecedents (son of a Boston captain of police), Joe has embraced a criminal lifestyle and is employed by one of the most ruthless of Boston's bootleggers. The life Joe has chosen is infused with betrayal and violence, and what pangs of conscience he has must be vigorously suppressed. But his struggle with his own bad faith and regret is tested as Joe (handling the bootleg business in Tampa) realises that the choices his father warned him of can no longer be avoided. What's more, Joe's beautiful, rebellious Cuban wife utilises the dirty money from his activities to save women of the streets – even as Joe finesses the very mechanisms that keep these women's lives in such a desperate state.

There are many things to praise here, not least the well-crafted period detail of Lehane's crowded narrative. There is also the author's typically acerbic command of language, a skill that seems to get better from book to book. If there is a problem with *Live By Night*, it is that the characters seem to be moved by the demands of the narrative rather than being individuals possessing the kind of teeming life that marked such books as *Mystic River* (Joe's crises of conscience have far less force than those to be found in that book). Nevertheless, Dennis Lehane aficionados will luxuriate in the persuasive storytelling here, and Lehane's grand-scale writing makes most contemporary crime fiction look footling and lacking in ambition.

DONNA LEON has long been the perfect conduit to Italy for a dedicated army of readers, and her Commissario Brunetti novels are an institution. Leon presents her adopted city, Venice, in all its aspects, from its beauty to its corruption, and that corruption stretches to the upper echelons of government. *About Face* boasts a complex and mystifying plot. A fellow *carabiniere*, Guarino, brings the Commissario into an ambitious investigation of Mafia takeovers of businesses in the Marghera region when the owner of a trucking company is found murdered in his offices – and Guarino believes the death is connected to the illegal transportation of refuse. Then Brunetti notices the odd, almost neurotic behaviour of his colleague. There are more elements than usual mixed into a labyrinthine plot here – and Leon shows, as ever, that she has the measure of the troubled soul of the city she lives in at her command.

PETER LEONARD knows that it's a double-edged sword being the son of one of the greatest of American crime writers, Elmore Leonard (the latter, sadly, not in this volume, as the focus is on contemporary living writers). Initially, of course, having a family name with such clout might get a tyro author published, but a son or daughter has to deliver the goods – which is what Peter Leonard has done with great authority over the course of several books. In fact, his style in such books as *All He Saw Was the Girl* is not really like his father's at all, although there is the same crackling, sardonic humour and dyspeptic view of the world. This may well be the book that sees him emerge decisively from his father's shadow – although, if the truth be told, he did that with his first book.

JOHN LESCROART worked as a musician before making a mark as a writer with *Son of Holmes*. His novel *Sunburn* (utilising his knowledge of Spain) enjoyed success, and his subsequent work has built him a solid reputation as one of the most reliable of current practitioners thanks to such books as *The Keeper*, which features his lawyer protagonist Dismas Hardy.

His publishers launched **JONATHAN LETHEM**'s *Motherless Brooklyn* in the UK with the *Newsweek* plaudits he had garnered: the author was named as one of the '100 People for the New Century'. To that they can add the Crime Writers' Association Gold Dagger the book picked up. If this means that readers will take up a writer new to them, that's all to the good, for this is a truly unique and flinty novel, shot through with sardonic humour and extremely quirky characterisation.

Lionel Essrog, aka the Human Freakshow, is a victim of Tourette's syndrome, with an uncontrollable impulse to declaim nonsense, touch all surfaces and other disturbing symptoms. And when a local tough guy and fixer, Frank Minna, adopts the adolescent protagonist (along with three other orphans from the St Vincent's Home for Boys) and educates them to become members of his close-to-the-edge detective agency, Lionel's life is changed irrevocably. But when Minna – known as the Secret Prince of Brooklyn – is savagely killed, Lionel is forced to become a real detective, and is soon up to his neck in the murky world in which Minna moved. It became a cliché for television detectives to be disabled in some fashion (blind, heavily overweight, wheelchair-bound, etc.), but any suspicions that Lethem will be going down that familiar path are soon ruthlessly expunged. The treatment of the protagonist's condition is both responsible and compelling, lending his narrative a hard-edged realism.

DAVID LEVIEN's *City of the Sun* was something of a find. The author is one of the most sought-after screenwriters in Hollywood – which does not, of course, guarantee skill as a novelist. The narrative here, which begins when a 12-year-old newspaper delivery boy vanishes on his route, quickly exerts a grip, and Levien is adroit at involving the reader in the plight of a very ordinary couple – the boy's parents – who hire a tough, recalcitrant ex-cop, Frank Behr, to help them in their desperate quest for their son. There are elements of Harlan Coben in the impressively handled plot here (and Coben lends his name to the enterprise with a jacket rave).

The achievement of **PAM LEWIS** in such books as *Speak Softly, She Can Hear* doesn't just lie in the well-honed suspense set pieces but in the layers of psychological menace. Carole Mason and her friend Naomi are teenagers who opt to have their first sexual encounter with the charismatic Eddie Lindbaeck. The experience results in a squalid death in a motel. Carole, overweight and naive, is persuaded by Eddie to conceal the crime – and is even made to feel responsible. The years pass, and Carole tries to put the past behind her. But then Eddie reappears and the edifice of her life threatens to collapse. There's a hint of Donna Tartt's *The Secret History* woven into Lewis's narrative, and though this American newcomer has aimed at a more commercial read, the literary-style prose is subtle and astringent, while Carole is a vividly drawn protagonist.

Are you a fan of one of the most outrageous shows on TV, *Dexter*? If you are, you have a taste for the darkest humour, as *Dexter* is not for those of a conventional mindset (or, for that matter, the squeamish). Dexter Morgan is an alienated serial killer – a psychopath who is barely in touch with everyday human emotion, and who relates to those around him with an outsider's eye. The twist, however – author **JEFF LINDSAY**'s masterstroke – is that Dexter is also a Miami cop, an expert on the bloodiest of murder scenes, and the killers he clandestinely eliminates are monsters, far worse (he thinks) than himself.

The third of Jeff Lindsay's novels was *Dexter in the Dark*. After the macabre delights of *Darkly Dreaming Dexter* and *Dearly Devoted Dexter*, its appearance was surely a cause for celebration, wasn't it? Well, yes... up to a point. Two Miami college students have been immolated and decapitated in ritualistic fashion, and at the grisly crime scene Dexter Morgan has a queasy realisation that he is up against a force more ruthless than the Dark Passenger, his own motivating inner voice. And then something happens that begins to change the shape of the narrative from anything Lindsay has done before: Dexter's Dark Passenger falls silent. Something else is to change Dexter's life: he is about to marry his fiancée (who has two young children, Astor and Cody) – more to provide cover for his homicidal activities than to turn him into a normal human being. The gruesome killings continue, and Lindsay gives the grim force behind the murders a name: 'It' (this is only the first of several reminders of Stephen King's supernatural horrors). All of this is as entertainingly idiosyncratic as usual, but the tone of the book is very different from its predecessors – not least for the puzzling absence for most of the novel of the Dark Passenger so effectively used in the earlier outings. Some readers may query Lindsay's decision to make Dexter's guiding force a supernatural being rather than just a metaphor for the more plausible psychosis resulting from the hideous death of his mother. But there are still quirky pleasures galore here, such as

Dexter's panicky dealings with his two newly acquired children, who take a very unhealthy interest in his bloody hobbies. Is he to have a couple of youthful apprentices?

In such thrillers as *In the Lake of the Moon* and *Requiem for a Glass Heart*, **DAVID LINDSEY** has shown himself to be a writer with a punchy yet elegantly textured style. He is strikingly good at torpedoing the clichés that accrue to the thriller protagonist, and in *The Colour of Night*, Harry Strand is a particularly felicitous creation. Harry is trying to forget his career in American intelligence and is struggling to come to terms with the tragic death of his wife in a car crash. He has reinvented himself as a successful art dealer, but his new life is ruptured when the seductive Mara Song comes to him with a beguiling proposition – to act as broker for her astonishing portfolio of sketches by modern masters. It's an offer he can't refuse, but when he discovers a video cassette at Mara's home that shows his wife's final moments of life as her car is forced off the road, he realises that the only thing that matters in his life is finding her killer – now within his grasp. By engaging us in Strand's problems so irresistibly, Lindsey is able to ensure that the mechanics of his plot move with relentless precision as his hero gets nearer and nearer to his wife's murderer.

Writers such as Gillian Flynn (with *Gone Girl*) and Paula Hawkins (with *The Girl on the Train*) may have caught the popular mood for 'domestic noir' and watched their sales rocket, but if there is any justice, **LAURA LIPPMAN** – who for years has been producing some of the best-written literary crime fiction on the contemporary scene – will soon be enjoying similar commercial success. She certainly deserves to – and *After I'm Gone* may be just the book to propel her from the middle to the upper slopes of Mount Parnassus. An Arcadian past was the subject of her much-lauded novel *The Innocents*; the past in *After I'm Gone*, however, is not just a different country but a dangerous one. In prose that is rich and complex, Lippman shows that the crime genre can be infinitely flexible in tackling its basic concerns – and a few new ones. The disparate time periods here would have been quicksand for lesser writers, but they are skilfully negotiated by Lippman as she describes the lives of five women whose happiness has been destroyed by Felix Brewer, a white-collar crook and adulterer who vanished in 1976, leaving chaos in his wake. The women are his wife Bambi, his mistress Julie and his three daughters, all of whom are strikingly characterised – as is Detective Roberto 'Sandy' Sanchez, investigating Julie's murder in the present day. Sanchez, a retired detective, uncovers a web of criminality, jealousy and avarice stretching over several decades and affecting the lives of these very different women. And even though so much time has passed, the missing conman is still crucial to the women's existence. But a reckoning – for everyone – is in the offing.

Anatomising a murky criminal past is meat and drink to writers of crime fiction, but few do it as well as Laura Lippman – and as well as conjuring the individual dilemmas of the women at the centre of *After I'm Gone*, she is particularly adroit at evoking a period when women were only starting to enjoy some autonomy. The locale, too, is vividly evoked: Lippman's own city of Baltimore. At times she draws us into a modern take on the dark atmosphere of one of her favourite writers who resided in the city, Edgar Allan Poe (Lippman has admitted to obsessively haunting Poe's old stamping grounds). But all of this would count for nothing if the plotting were not as rigorous and impressive as it is here: as Sanchez draws ever closer to the truth, it will be a very seasoned crime reader indeed who will be able to see the twists coming before they spring out.

After the publishing phenomenon that was **ROBERT LITTELL**'s *The Company*, the author was always going to find that book a hard act to follow. One of the achievements of the novel was to touch upon a host of important historical events, all conjured with maximum vividness. In *Legends*, Littell shifted his attention from the Cold War panoply of the earlier book to the dangerous life of a lone CIA operative who finds himself in a maelstrom of betrayal. *A Nasty Piece of Work* is a relatively slim volume for Littell (coming in at under 260 pages), but it is as finely honed a thriller as any aficionado might wish for. Ex-CIA agent Lemuel Gunn has left his profession behind him, swapping the bloodshed of Afghanistan for a cramped trailer in New Mexico and hopefully undertaking a new career as a private investigator. But his first case involves a woman called Ornella Neppi who is inexorably running her uncle's bail bonds business into the ground. Ornella enlists Gunn's aid when a criminal called Emilio Gava jumps bail after an arrest for cocaine buying. But things (unsurprisingly) prove to be radically different from the initial impressions that Gunn has of the case.

Those fearing that Littell has left his espionage comfort zone behind for the territory of the tough private eye novel need not hesitate: Gunn is a winning protagonist, and *A Nasty Piece of Work* is every bit as richly characterised, quirky and mesmerising as his more usual fare.

A warning: you should never ask a crime fiction reviewer what you should be reading. They will freeze like rabbits in the headlights and suffer an instant politician-type brain fade. Personally, I have one name that is my default response whenever I'm pinned down in this fashion: **ATTICA LOCKE**.

To say that her debut *Black Water Rising* – ambitious, socially committed and beautifully written – created a stir is almost to understate the case, and one wondered if it weighed heavily on her shoulders that she would be obliged to deliver something equally impressive as a follow-up. She did just that with *The Cutting Season*, and, subsequently, *Pleasantville*. The latter is set in 1996. In Houston, a mayoral election is in the offing, and a key swing area is the African-American neighbourhood of Pleasantville. The district has swung every race since it was created in 1949 to house a burgeoning black middle class. The nomination of Houston's mayor seems to be assured: Axel Hathorne has the perfect pedigree. He is an ex-chief of police and the son of the district's founding father, Sam Hathorne, so he is an obvious winner. But Axel learns that one should not count one's chickens. A late entrant in the mayoral competition is defence attorney Sandy Wolcott, who has achieved fame after a much-publicised murder trial. And then things begin to get considerably worse for Axel: with the competition at white heat, a girl canvassing for Axel disappears, and when her body is discovered, Axel's nephew is charged with the murder. The older Hathorne, Sam, is keen for Jay Porter (who we first encountered in *Black Water Rising*) to defend his grandson – even though Jay is reluctant to do it. He has grown disenchanted with his job, despite the great financial success he has enjoyed. But his attempts to stay out of the courtroom are doomed to failure; a truly seismic court case is about to change the lives of everyone involved and expose the venality of some powerful people.

Those holding their breath to see if Locke can match the achievement of her earlier books can exhale – *Pleasantville* is every inch as impressive as its predecessors, with a new nuance and complexity burnishing the narrative. As in her earlier work, awkward political issues bristle at the edges, such as the black families who have achieved some success finding themselves at odds with the resentful Latino families undertaking a vain search for the same advantages. And Jay, increasingly out of his depth in a powder keg situation, remains a satisfyingly conflicted character. The sultry, edgy atmosphere of the town is reminiscent of one of the American masters of crime fiction, James Lee Burke – and this appears to be no accident, as Locke names the family of the murdered girl 'Robicheaux' (the surname of Burke's durable sleuth). But Locke is moving in different territory, notably that of the riveting courtroom drama – and at that particular discipline, she is the equal of such writers as John Grisham.

So the next time you find yourself in the company of a crime reviewer, don't bother asking who you should be reading. You already know at least one simple two-word answer: Attica Locke.

ERIC VAN LUSTBADER's publishers years ago dropped the 'Van' from his name so that he would be alphabetically higher on bookshop shelves; that ploy has long since been abandoned, and the author has the 'Van' back. But whatever name he writes under, he is one of the most reliable of thriller writers in the field, as *The Testament* shows. Bravo Shaw's father dies under strange circumstances, and the secrets that Bravo always knew his father possessed come to light. Dexter Shaw belonged to a clandestine religious cult, long thought to have been banished. The sect have a lost testament that could bring an end to Christianity... and Bravo is soon on their trail.

LISA LUTZ is the author of such novels as *The Passenger* and the popular Spellman series, along with work in children's books, while also penning the gangster comedy *Plan B*, a film she disliked. Lutz has won the Alex Award and has been nominated for the Edgar Award for best novel.

One of the reasons why readers go back to the thriller genre again and again is the delicious pleasure of plotting: nothing exhilarates more than some ingenious and surprising narrative, and that's something **PHILLIP MARGOLIN** delivers with such books as *Ties That Bind* – and in spades. Lawyer Amanda Jaffe is saddled with a case that makes her feel she's up against insuperable odds: her client is facing execution and has just killed his own lawyer. Jon Dupre is, self-evidently, a nasty piece of work: a wheeler and dealer in the dirty world of selling both drugs and women, and his fate is clearly sealed. But as Amanda digs beneath the surface of the case, she finds herself with the proverbial can of worms: Dupre can claim friends in the most unlikely of places – and not just at the criminal end of society. He is the custodian of some very dark secrets, and before he starts spilling them there are people who will go to considerable lengths to maintain the status quo. Apart from the satisfyingly convoluted narrative, Margolin's skill here (already evident in earlier books, such as *The Burning Man* and *The Associate*) lies in the creation of a strongly drawn, conflicted protagonist – and Amanda is certainly that. We've met her type before, but Margolin rings the changes with aplomb.

MARGARET MARON was born in North Carolina, where the piedmont meets the sand hills, and grew up on a modest two-mule tobacco farm that had been in her family for over a hundred years. Her first serious work consisted of tales about NYPD Lieutenant Sigrid Harald, novels set against the New York City art world. Living there allowed the author to see the city as a collection of villages, each with its own identity. After returning to North Carolina, she created District Court Judge Deborah Knott, the opinionated daughter of an ex-bootlegger and youngest sibling of 11 older brothers.

Gillian Flynn, author of the monster hit *Gone Girl*, adorns the jacket of **BECKY MASTERMAN**'s *Fear the Darkness* with an enthusiastic endorsement, so attention must be paid – and such previous Masterman books as *Rage Against the Dying* certainly suggest that this one will justify readers' time. Ex-FBI agent Brigid Quinn is hoping for a second chance in life, having quit the Bureau for what she fondly hopes will be a normal life. 'No more serial killers' is her wish, just a pleasant married existence. But when the mother of a teenager who has drowned in a tragic accident turns to her for help, her old skills are called upon again. Which is invariably the case in novels such as this – the past has a long reach. But Becky Masterman keeps the story fresh and involving.

In *Abandoned* by **CODY MCFADYEN**, Special Agent Smoky Barrett's speciality is tracking down the most dangerous and unhinged of criminals. One case has a particularly personal application for her: at the wedding of her best friend, a woman is thrown from a car, the victim of imprisonment and torture. But why has her tormentor chosen to set her free at the church during a wedding where most of those present are police officers? As Barrett and her team begin to investigate, they realise that they are on the trail of a particularly brilliant psychopath.

MICHAEL MCGARRITY holds degrees in psychology and clinical social work, and his subsequent career in criminal justice included work in corrections, law enforcement and security, as well as a spell as a Santa Fe County deputy sheriff. With his novel *Tularosa* in 1996, McGarrity turned to writing full-time. The author's inventive Kevin Kerney series, set in New Mexico, has a dedicated following and has changed over the years, moving from classic Westerns to books about the career of a modern police chief.

Since the success of *Primary Colors*, White House-connected *romans à clef* have become a hot item, but *The First Counsel* is the first time the concept has been successfully welded on to the thriller format. Actually, though, the real-life references are less important than **BRAD MELTZER**'s smooth handling of an ingenious plot. 'Shadow' is the Secret Service code name for the president's daughter, Nora Hartson. Young White House lawyer Michael Garrick discovers that there are side effects to dating the First Daughter, and they are not all desirable. On one of their dates, Nora and Michael witness something that they shouldn't see, and, in order to protect her, Michael begins a process of cover-up that soon plunges him into nightmare. The reader is in familiar territory here: the hero who can turn to no one for aid. Meltzer is another lawyer-turned-novelist, with all that implies – but the pacey writing and well-turned characterisation lift this one well out of the workaday, and the relationship between Michael and the unhappy Nora is treated intelligently, adding another cachet of quality.

The theme of the Wandering Jew is one that has to be handled sensitively these days, but it has inspired artists from Goethe to Dumas: a rootless man forced to live in alien lands and unable to expiate some nameless sin. The concept clearly still has mileage, as Bostonian writer **DEREK B MILLER**'s bravura *Norwegian by Night* proves. Miller's unhappy Jewish anti-hero is an 82-year-old American called Sheldon, on the brink of senility, fearing the demons of his past and ill at ease in his new country, Norway – despite the fact that his long-suffering granddaughter Rhea and her Scandinavian husband Lars do their damnedest to accommodate him. This short-fused ex-New Yorker harbours a paranoid fear that relatives of the Koreans he killed in the Korean War will seek him out to murder him. Miller allows Sheldon to stand in for every alienated outsider in the modern world, raging against his own country while failing to get a handle on the foreigners who surround him.

Miller's debut has a range of concerns, but central is the place of the Jew in a hostile modern world. So, Bernard Malamud/Philip Roth/ Saul Bellow territory, surely? But by Chapter 3, we find ourselves deep in Nordic noir territory, with murder, brutal Balkan villains and a frantic cross-country chase the order of the day. Spying on his quarrelling neighbours, Sheldon invites a young woman ('everything about her says *Balkans*') with her six-year-old son into his apartment when she is threatened by her husband and sinister-looking men parked in a car nearby. But the rescue attempt ends in the death of the woman, and soon the elderly Sheldon is on the run with the silent boy, whom he names Paul; the boy reminds him of his own dead son, Saul. The incongruous couple, with the young Norwegian 'Paul' wearing a toy Viking helmet, are soon on a dangerous odyssey – one that takes place as much in the mind of its tetchy protagonist (plagued by flashbacks to when he was a sniper – or perhaps not) as it does in the real world. Is *Norwegian by Night* another entry in the Scandicrime genre or a literary piece dipping its toe into those remunerative waters? Either way, it is a remarkable debut, burnished with some incisive writing as it describes its weighty themes of national and racial identity. More than enough, in fact, to make us forget the odd infelicity.

Clean Cut was an auspicious debut thriller for **THERESA MONSOUR**, and *Cold Blood* delivered more complex and well-honed diversion. Once again, characterisation is a key element: Monsour is canny enough to draw us into her characters so that the tense storytelling exerts the requisite grip. A search has been mounted for Bunny Pederson, who has vanished after acting as a bridesmaid at a friend's wedding. A salesman, Trip, who has volunteered to help in the search, discovers a severed finger, but the case remains one of habeas corpus. Minneapolis detective Paris Murphy remembers Trip from her school – and he has been involved with a previous case. Her marriage in trouble, and a faltering affair to cope with, Paris doesn't need to get involved. But, of course, she does – with dangerous results. Shades of Michael Connelly haunt a dark and atmospheric piece.

In such books as the tense *Play Dead*, the capable **RICHARD MONTANARI** has proved himself a master of the pulse-pounding novel of suspense; a relatively unsung master in the UK, perhaps (despite the best efforts over the years of his British publisher), his profile remains stubbornly low key, despite respectable sales. Fellow practitioners such as James Ellroy and Tess Gerritsen have sung his praises – and *The Devil's Garden* enjoyed a similar chorus of approval.

While **CHRIS MOONEY**'s persuasive and edgy thriller *Deviant Ways* may recycle familiar elements from the now overcrowded serial killer genre, it does so with imagination and invention. After all, there are so many dogged cops with fragile private lives stalking – and being stalked by – grimly ingenious psychotics, it's impossible to avoid certain ideas popping up again and again. The real question remains: can an author make the material seem fresh? Largely speaking, Mooney pulls off the trick with real panache, and his troubled FBI profiler hero Jack Casey is a very plausible protagonist, even if his struggle with a life shattered by an earlier encounter with a psychopath is one we know well from many another thriller. His nemesis is The Sandman, a terrifyingly prescient madman who is slaughtering not just one individual at a time, but whole families and whole neighbourhoods. His method is explosives (shades of the Oklahoma bombings), and he knows quite as much about Jack Casey as he does about his well-researched victims – particularly how to really twist the knife in his FBI opposite number. Mooney kicks off with a joltingly orchestrated prelude, and the simmering threat of appalling violence keeps the reader transfixed throughout. Unless you've a serious case of serial killer fatigue (and many of us have), this is definitely one for the shopping list.

DAVID MORRELL is the award-winning author of *First Blood*, the novel in which his protagonist Rambo first appeared. The character's notoriety is, of course, based on the increasingly unsubtle series of films starring Sylvester Stallone and the lazy UK tabloid journalism; the latter speciously invoked Rambo as inspiration for some real-life murders in Britain. But that first David Morrell book is quite a different experience from the films, and at a meal in London for the author, I put it to him that his novel's brilliant evocation of place and survival in a rural setting was reminiscent of the Geoffrey Household gone-to-earth classic *Rogue Male*. 'Absolutely!' replied Morrell. 'That's one of my favourite books, and if I can be compared favourably to Geoffrey Household, I am more than pleased.' In fact, Morrell knows the crime and thriller genre well, and with Declan Burke he edited an entertaining volume of essays on his fellow practitioners, *Books To Die For*. Morrell (actually born in Canada) is also the co-founder of the International Thriller Writers organisation and is considered by many to be the father of the modern action novel.

The unfamiliarity of a writer's name should not put off potential buyers, and evidence of this is the fact that **BOYD MORRISON** proves to be a particularly adept novelist, with a notable skill for raising the pulse of the reader; every page of *The Catalyst* demonstrates this. Doctor Michael Ward dies in a suspicious fire, and his student Kevin Hamilton believes it was no accident. The young PhD student received an email from Ward before the blaze, warning him that their recent experiment has led to one of the most important discoveries of the century: a chemical process with the potential to destroy global industries.

WALTER MOSLEY and George Pelecanos are two writers who don't make life easy for their liberal (small 'l') white readers – which is a tad unfair, as the redneck racists who are the real targets of their anger are highly unlikely to be dipping into their books. But if the readers who have made the duo the most respected in contemporary American crime fiction are to be discomfited by the scalding tone of their writing when it comes to race (most non-black individuals in their books share a common racial guilt), perhaps that's the price to be paid for the way certain Caucasians behave.

However, while both authors foreground black protagonists in their work, only one of them is black: Mosley, who in the much-acclaimed Easy Rawlins series (notably *Devil in a Blue Dress*) has created a dazzling sequence of gritty and epigrammatic latter-day riffs on Raymond Chandler.

Mosley's *Little Scarlet* is set immediately after the devastating Los Angeles riots of 1965 that divided the city along racial lines. Black people are at the receiving end of brutal police beatings, while anyone with a white skin is likely to be beaten by angry blacks. Such a man, pulled from his car by a mob during the riots, dashes for safety into a nearby apartment. Shortly afterwards, a woman known as Little Scarlet is found brutally murdered, with the target victim of the mob apparently responsible. Easy Rawlins finds himself dropped into this incandescent situation when the police ask for his help. They fear that their presence could bring back the chaos of the riots, and feel that Easy might be able to track down the missing man. Reluctantly, he agrees, and discovers that the killer is a man motivated by a similar rage to that which courses through his own veins. This is Mosley firing on all cylinders, and it's always good to see the familiar tropes of the hard-boiled novel given a fresh airing: the enticing teenage Juanda, keen to bed Easy, is closely related to the various nymphets Philip Marlowe found between his sheets. (Easy, like Marlowe on such occasions, keeps his pants on.)

But while *Little Scarlet* functions unerringly on the level of a tough and idiomatic detective thriller, the author's personal resentment at the treatment of African Americans smoulders as keenly as that of his protagonist; the events described here may have taken place in 1965, but Mosley clearly sees them as completely contemporary. Easy doesn't want the mob violence, but he is tired of policemen stopping him for just walking down the street: 'What good was law and order if it meant I was supposed to ignore the fact that our children were treated like little hoodlums and whores?'

Some crime writers are happy turning out straightforward genre products that work on the simple level of delivering thrills, and there's certainly nothing wrong with that. But writers such as Mosley are clearly constrained by the demands of crime writing, and each book is an attempt to widen the boundaries of what is permissible within the genre. In fact, for some time, Mosley has been regarded as one of the writers whose work often strays into the realms of literature. And when you add this to a vision that incorporates an uncompromising picture of black life, the result is powerful stuff indeed. *Walkin' the Dog* has come to be regarded as a controversial Mosley novel: some consider it to be among his very best work, but there are those who feel that the broadening out of the characterisation here slightly sidelines the narrative. Whatever your view, few would deny that this is one of the most hard-edged and intelligent pieces of crime writing you are likely to encounter. Mosley's protagonist Socrates Fortlow (who first appeared in *Always Outnumbered, Always Outgunned*) is struggling to come to terms with life after prison. He has a two-room shack in Watts, a relationship, and even a job. But, as so often in this kind of narrative, the past won't leave him alone, and Socrates has to risk everything he's achieved to bring down some savage and corrupt enemies. Ghetto life has rarely been delivered with such a dark panache, and Socrates is one of the most vividly realised of Mosley's protagonists.

It is a time-honoured tradition of crime and thriller fiction to leave a protagonist for dead at the end of a book, whetting the appetite for a possible resurrection. Lee Child has appeared to kill off Jack Reacher, and, in an earlier era, James Bond slid to the floor at the end of *From Russia, with Love* after an apparently fatal poisoning, courtesy of Rosa Klebb's shoes. When Walter Mosley tried a similar tactic at the end of *Blonde Faith*, the 'final' outing for his battered and cynical hero Easy Rawlins, readers may not have been persuaded that they had seen the last of one of the most distinctive characters in modern crime fiction. And, with *Little Green*, they were proved right. Superlatives are routinely flung around by publishers, but few would argue with the fact that Mosley is comfortably the finest living black writer in the crime genre, even if his followers have felt of late that his flame has been burning low – as is so often the case with prolific writers (Mosley has over 40 books to his credit). But *Little Green* represents Mosley on typically acerbic and exhilarating form, evoking such classics as his signature novel, *Devil in a Blue Dress*.

At the beginning of this book, Rawlins wakes up from the coma he was in at the end of *Blonde Faith*, but instead of a period of recuperation, he is quickly handed a pressing new investigation: a friend's son is missing. Without much delay, we are once again sampling the fleshpots of Sunset Boulevard, from the upmarket clubs to the squalid LSD dens. The solution to the mystery lies in a benighted past – in this case, the counterculture of the 1960s.

Easy Rawlins has been described as a black Philip Marlowe, but a more apposite parallel might be the saturnine sleuth created by Ross Macdonald, Lew Archer, similarly prone to finding that familial flaws (rather than venality) are the source of malign behaviour. As ever with Mosley, the narrative is set against a picturesquely drawn Los Angeles, with the tapestry of American history always as significant as the violent activities of the protagonists. The siren call of drugs is examined dispassionately here, but not so race, which remains an incendiary element, and perhaps the one that most energises a writer who is as much a social critic as an entertainer.

Detroit native **MARCIA MULLER** self-published three copies of her first novel (with a canine subject) when she was only 12. At the beginning of the 1970s, she started to write mystery novels, her first success coming with *Edwin of the Iron Shoes*, the inaugural novel featuring San Francisco private investigator Sharon McCone. The second McCone novel, *Ask the Cards a Question*, was to be followed by over 35 novels, some of them written in collaboration with her husband, the writer Bill Pronzini. In 2005, Muller was named a Grand Master by Mystery Writers of America, the organisation's highest award. Pronzini received this accolade in 2008, making them only the second couple to share the award (the other being Margaret Millar and Ross Macdonald).

The Artie Cohen novels of **REGGIE NADELSON** customarily furnish sardonic, idiosyncratic reads, but *Manhattan 62* has bigger fish to fry. 1962. A young Cuban is discovered on a railroad, grotesquely mutilated, the second murder in New York that has left its victim with a tattoo of a worm and the words 'Cuba Libre'. Irish NYPD detective Pat Wynne has a politically sensitive case on his hands with espionage a possible element – and minds are concentrated by the fact that Cuban missiles are trained on America. The tension is palpable. Nadelson is fascinated by the atmosphere of political paranoia of the period, but there is also a loving celebration of early 1960s New York in which discussion and debate are endemic. As ever with this writer, the sense of place is crucial, but what really energises the narrative here is the political turmoil, ever present in both the characters' minds and the reader's.

Nadelson's crime series featuring Moscow-born New Yorker Artie Cohen has built up a considerable following, with such books as *Red Mercury Blues* and *Bloody London* full of the quirky, irreverent writing that is Nadelson's stock in trade. *Sex Dolls* strikes out into new territory in its unflinching depiction of a snowbound Paris in thrall to a grim trade in sex slaves. Artie Cohen, disturbed by changes in his long-term girlfriend Lily, is summoned from London to Paris, where he finds that Lily has been savagely raped and beaten in an unused apartment. Her amnesia offers Artie few clues, and he has no choice but to investigate a very seamy side of Paris, one little known to the tourists. Artie's interest in jazz and the darker side of life is not, he finds, sufficient preparation for the world of abused hookers and human enslavement he finds. And as his search for Lily's attackers leads him into considerable danger, he is pitched into a truly international trade that takes no prisoners. New York-born Nadelson, who lives in London, has created a strongly drawn, engaging protagonist in the womanising Artie, and his encounters with the various lowlifes of *Sex Dolls* makes for scabrous and involving reading. The pace of the book is ever accelerating, with Artie's cross-country investigations exerting a considerable grip. Nadelson is good, too, on the various locales of the novel; from London to Paris, Vienna to New York, all of Artie's destinations are etched with colour and atmosphere. If *Hot Poppies* remains the most gripping Artie Cohen entry, this one runs it a close second.

VIET THANH NGUYEN, Associate Professor of English and American Studies and Ethnicity at the University of Southern California, is the author of the novel *The Sympathizer*, perhaps closer to the espionage than the crime genre, which won the 2016 Pulitzer Prize for Fiction, an Edgar Award for best first novel from the Mystery Writers of America, and a slew of other awards. More typical of his output, perhaps, is *Nothing Ever Dies: Vietnam and the Memory of War*, the critical adjunct to a project whose fictional bookend is the novel mentioned above.

CAROL O'CONNELL is the creator of Kathy Mallory, the distinctive detective who features in the majority of her books; *It Happens in the Dark* is one of the most memorable, and the books have gleaned bushels of praise. In *Winter House*, a serial killer is discovered at the eponymous house with shears sticking out of his chest, and NYPD detective Kathy Mallory is called in to investigate. But she realises that the first person in the frame clearly did not commit the crime.

A good introduction (for those who need it) to both O'Connell and Mallory.

SARA PARETSKY's VI Warshawski remains the most distinctive female private investigator in American crime fiction, and her continuing survival – after numerous pummellings, both physical and emotional – is somehow both plausible and (for readers) very welcome. Cover-ups and conspiracies are familiar Warshawski territory, along with keen, fiery social commitment. Destructive family secrets often crop up; families can be threatening places in VI's minatory world, repeatedly echoing Philip Larkin's view of what our mothers and fathers do to us. And often in Paretsky's hefty books, the emotional involvement of her detective in the cases is both ill-advised and inevitable. There is also a keen sense of loss: the slow, melancholy demise of the American dream and the optimistic ideals of Paretsky's baby boomer generation – which is not to say that the books aren't always exhilarating and utterly involving.

Brush Back is set in her familiar stamping ground of South Chicago, with Vic Warshawski revisiting an old neighbourhood (and a teenage boyfriend) she left years before. Her old flame, Frank Guzzo, enlists her reluctant aid in a difficult problem. His mother Stella has served several decades in prison for killing Frank's sister Annie, a crime of which she claims to be innocent. VI's reluctance to help is based on the unconcealed dislike that Stella had towards the Warshawski family, but things move up a notch when Stella names VI's late cousin, a hockey player (murdered in an earlier Paretsky book) as being involved in the crime. Now obliged to clear a relative's name, Warshawski finds herself – as so often before – in the fraught territory of political corruption and equally vicious neighbourhood resentments.

Paretsky's sleuth manages to rile even more people in *Brush Back* than usual, and remains as bloody-minded as ever. The wide-ranging canvas here covers everything from her own tangled personal history to murders from the past, Chicago history, ruthless gangsters and the implacable demands of family. It's rich and aromatic, immensely entertaining – although the various baseball references (Paretsky is a fan) will be lost on most British readers.

Much acclaimed for her nonpareil detective fiction, Paretsky is also famous for her views on serious issues: the rise of religious fundamentalism in her own country, the Iraq war, the erosion of women's rights, infringements on all our personal liberties. And without ever allowing her fiction to proselytise, such concerns give her books provocative undercurrents that elevate them above more quotidian crime fiction. Identity, too, is a theme: not just of the murdered Annie (was she the likable ambitious girl VI remembers, or the cynical, amoral woman Stella claims she was?), but also the character of Victoria Iphigenia herself, never quite fixed, always somehow alienated from those around her.

Paretsky, born in Ames, Iowa in 1947, spent her childhood in Kansas in an isolated house with her perpetually quarrelling parents; her father was the first Jewish academic to secure a tenured position at the University of Kansas. The family lived out of town as they were *personae non gratae* in many places. After completing a PhD in history at the University of Chicago and gaining an MBA in business studies, Paretsky began to write her detective fiction, in which she created the most significant female private eye in the history of the genre, VI Warshawski. Her protagonist, while tough and resourceful, customarily – and ill-advisedly – becomes emotionally involved in most of her cases. Chicago, VI's beat, is evocatively conjured in book after book, which tackle many cutting-edge social issues. Paretsky is married to a professor of physics, and has lived in Chicago since the 1960s.

T JEFFERSON PARKER had written (by 2016) 22 California-set crime novels after his debut in the 1980s, and Parker has achieved the rare feat of bagging three Edgar Awards (two for best novel, which is rare in itself, and a third Edgar Award for a short story). His debut, *Laguna Heat*, was turned into an HBO movie, and he has also won the *LA Times* Book Prize and has been nominated for the Anthony, Macavity and Barry Awards and the prestigious Hammett Prize.

'Why do you Brits always pick on my short chapters?' **JAMES PATTERSON** is apt to say in mock exasperation to British interviewers: 'Nobody in the States ever brings the subject up!' Diplomatic Brits usually refrain from making pithy comments about the respective attention span of British and American readers; even if we did, Patterson could point to his phenomenal sales – on both sides of the Atlantic – and dissent is firmly routed. The author knows precisely how to manipulate his readers – and despite recurring criticism of the pared-down chapters, that unyielding grip is precisely what his admirers cite as the reason for Patterson's success. The creator of the Alex Cross novels has been besting the sales of his confrères in the crime-writing field for many a moon, and the utilitarian prose really gets the job done.

Patterson's *Honeymoon* (one of the many books he has co-authored, this time with the less well-known Howard Roughan) has all the familiar Patterson traits: satisfyingly tortuous plotting and a narrative trajectory that never pauses for breath. FBI Agent John O'Hara is drawn with economical skill, as is his growing sexual obsession with the bewitching Nora Sinclair (a woman with whom it is unlucky to have any kind of relationship). This has elements of Hitchcock's *Vertigo* (or perhaps even the Boileau and Narcejac original), and its page-turning quality is *sui generis*. If the Patterson book lacks the pithy character observation that distinguishes many other writers' work, that may be due to the adulterated nature of *Honeymoon*, which bears signs of a plot synopsis by Patterson worked up into a novel by the less talented Roughan. The literary ventriloquism, however, is still pretty persuasive.

In *The Spire* by **RICHARD NORTH PATTERSON**, a youthful college president has vowed to save his alma mater, Caldwell College, from a financial scandal linked to the murder of a student that took place many years before. The most significant landmark on the college campus is the bell tower known as the Spire. It was at the foot of this tower that the body of Angela Hall, a young student, was discovered, raped and murdered. Patterson's efficiency at delivering his well-turned novels is celebrated. He is one of the legion of trial lawyers who have turned to thriller writing, but in his case the change of career was extremely good news for readers of intelligent thrillers.

CHRIS PAVONE's debut novel, *The Expats*, knocked readers on their ear with its superbly plotted, surprise-packed authority, and it is a pleasure to find that its follow-up, *The Accident*, is every bit as accomplished. Here, Pavone draws on his long experience as a publisher – and he puts his knowledge to good use in his heroine, top of the tree in her profession. *The Accident* is a hectically paced, very topical thriller that takes place over the course of a single day when a highly dangerous document throws the lives of a literary agent and an espionage operative into turmoil. Isabel Reed is one of New York's most high-powered literary agents, with a particularly impressive client list. But she comes across a manuscript that is unlike anything she has ever read before – and it keeps her reading into the wee small hours. The manuscript is hand-delivered anonymously, and Isabel finds it full of astonishing revelations and destabilising truths, with even the nation's security at potential risk. But she is torn by a dilemma: this could be the book that she has spent her entire career looking for, one that will transform the publishing industry – and, what's more, bring about a change in her life, which, despite her success, has been unhappy. At the same time, in Copenhagen, a seasoned station chief, Hayden Gray, is out of step with his bosses who see all threats to world peace coming from the Middle East. But Hayden has been keeping a weather eye on dangerous individuals in Europe. He knows all about the manuscript that Isabel has come into possession of, and is well aware that its contents are incendiary. He will do practically anything to make sure it never sees the light of day – and so begins a duel between the publishing agent and the secret operative, with both straining to outwit the other. And there is a third person in the equation: the enigmatic, anonymous author of the manuscript, with an unfathomable agenda. Within 24 fraught hours, some may live and some may die – and the Western world may be changed irrevocably. This is thriller writing for grown-ups, shot through with keen intelligence. It is not just a strong successor to *The Expats*, but a complex and involving novel in its own right. With just three books so far, Chris Pavone has put himself in the upper echelons of the pulse-racing fraternity.

RIDLEY PEARSON was the first American to receive the Raymond Chandler Fulbright Fellowship at Oxford University in 1990, and he has also received the Quill Award from the Missouri Writers Hall of Fame. His novels for adults include those featuring the characters John Knox and Grace Chu, including *The Red Room*, *Choke Point* and *The Risk Agent*, as well as a series with his protagonist Walt Fleming – *In Harm's Way*, *Killer Summer*, *Killer View* and *Killer Weekend* – along with many other novels, including his popular writing for young readers.

GEORGE PELECANOS is white (though with adopted black children) but shares black writer Walter Mosley's cold-eyed view of American society's treatment of race – although both men have a certain sympathy for those white men prepared to behave honourably in the face of the prejudice and incomprehension of their fellows. In this regard, while both share a left-of-centre view of society, they are not a million miles away from the social amelioration of Charles Dickens: it's not so much a change in the very nature of society that is required, but simply that men should behave well.

One of the reasons for George Pelecanos's reputation is his on-the-nail evocation of modern idioms: the gritty, pungent America he paints makes most of his contemporaries seem pale. And there's the soundtrack of his books: the carefully referenced popular music cues that his characters move to is a unique touch, although this built-in soundtrack has recently become a self-conscious device, with the novels seeming more and more like an iPod shopping list. It was good to see that element played down in *Drama City* – which was Pelecanos's best in some time. Lorenzo Brown has left his criminal background behind and is scratching a living in Washington as a dog warden. His parole officer, Rachel Lopez, discovers that Lorenzo, despite his good intentions, is turning out to be her biggest problem. Like Mosley, Pelecanos has limited hope for either social justice or a rapprochement between the races, but both writers have produced books that crackle with a visceral energy.

To the crime aficionado, Pelecanos is in a class of his own; he may not match, say, John Grisham's astronomical sales, but his gritty and astringent narratives are considered to be more rewarding than those of his better-known confrère. Initially, *Hell to Pay*, George Pelecanos's second book to feature black private investigator Derek Strange and his white colleague Terry Quinn, signals that it may be more interested in digging into the messy emotional lives of its tough heroes, but Pelecanos has wider aims. The hard-boiled scenario on offer here is really a frame for a piece of scabrous sociological writing, in which urban deprivation darkens the future of generations of young black males. Pelecanos has written cogently before about the cycle of violence that cripples the potential of so many young men, and his anger has a keen personal edge. Here, his two tarnished heroes become involved in the death of a youth, gunned down as an innocent bystander in a drug shooting, and Strange feels he must take out the killers in bloody ghetto fashion. But he's forced to confront some unpalatable truths about himself. His colleague Quinn, in the meantime, is dangerously involved in the world of teenage hookers and drug addicts and takes on the responsibility of a young girl in thrall to a vicious pimp. The writing at times has a genuinely epic quality, with an excoriating analysis of the dark underbelly of society echoing both Dostoyevsky and Nelson Algren. The bizarre juxtaposition of privilege and decay that is the city of Washington DC has rarely been anatomised as acutely as here (drug lord Granville Oliver is given the gravitas and influence of one of Washington's uptown senators), but the author's rage at times overburdens the demands of the thriller narrative. *Hell to Pay*, with its political agenda, sometimes comes across as Émile Zola wearing Raymond Chandler's trench coat.

Many writers excel at the well-turned acerbic thriller, but few are able to combine the tough dialogue and bloodletting with a massively ambitious picture of a whole society – and that's what Pelecanos achieves, time and time again. Do you want sardonic black humour? A thronging cast of vividly drawn protagonists, at war with themselves and their society? Pelecanos is your man. But for those who want their novels to take on heavier issues, Pelecanos's novels offer food for the brain along with pacey narratives. The author is a Greek-American with fingers in many pies (such as independent film production, notably the Coen Brothers' movies and writing duties on the cult series *The Wire*), and his first books (featuring investigator Nick Stefanos) quickly established his name, with popular music references that are a Pelecanos trademark peppered throughout the texts. But with the introduction of his black former cop Derek Strange (now a private investigator), Pelecanos moved on to a new, more rarefied stratum. The reader is given an astonishingly detailed picture of the whole of Washington society but with a concentration of the lowlife: gangsters, pimps, drug dealers and the tough cops who have to deal with them. The Derek Strange novels such as *Right as Rain* present unflinching pictures of Strange's work as an investigator after his stint on the force, but *Hard Revolution* takes us in a new direction: it is the spring of 1968, and Martin Luther King is attempting to preach his message of non-violent change to young blacks who are seething with impatience. Washington DC is a hotbed of resentment – and Derek Strange is at the start of his police career, dealing with both the casual racism of his cop colleagues and the very different route that his brother Dennis is taking. Dennis, after a period in the military, is drifting into bad company. Derek and his white partner, Troy Peters, are handling the callous thrill-killing of a young black man, as, elsewhere in the city, the elements of a robbery are slowly coalescing. Then King is assassinated and all hell breaks loose. The fashion in which Pelecanos counterpoints small-scale crime against national disaster is powerfully handled, though perhaps one of Strange's later assignments may be a better entry point for those new to Pelecanos.

The peripatetic **TWIST PHELAN** writes while travelling, and her work has been praised by such luminaries as Michael Connelly, Sue Grafton and Margaret Maron. After saying goodbye to a successful law career, Phelan sailed the globe in her own boat, and wrote such books as the popular Finn Teller mystery series.

GARY PHILLIPS has written both crime and graphic novels. The author (who grew up in South Central Los Angeles) has always loved comics, classic pulp and detective fiction, all of which fed into his first series character, Ivan Monk, in the early 1990s, a private detective at large in the racial tensions of contemporary California. Phillips' second series character, Martha Chainey, first appeared in *High Hand*, and he has written several standalones such as *The Jook*.

SCOTT PHILLIPS was much acclaimed for his debut novel, *The Ice Harvest*, which won the California Book Award and was a finalist for the Edgar Awards, the Hammett Prize and the Anthony Award. The book was successfully adapted for the cinema by Harold Ramis. Its follow-ups, *The Walkaway* and *Cottonwood*, also gleaned good reviews. Born in Wichita, Kansas, where much of his first two books are set, the author lived for many years in Paris, and then in Southern California, where he worked on screenplays.

Is **JODI PICOULT** a crime novelist? Let's be generous and include her here. In a career as successful as hers, it's difficult to pick one key book – but some provocative issues are suggested by *Mercy*. A man arrives at the police station in a Massachusetts town with the body of a woman whom he claims is his wife. He has killed her. He is immediately arrested by Cameron (Cam) MacDonald, a man who has a clear idea of what it means to be a force for law and order. Cam's wife is utterly devoted to him, but the couple's marriage is put under stress as the demands of justice become ever more difficult to fulfil. Cam finds that his life has become a moral quagmire in which he betrays his wife. This is a remarkably well-written book, with both a narrative that exerts a considerable grip and a readiness to confront complex moral issues (including that of a man who has brought about the death of his terminally ill wife). For the British reader, the book offers an insight into a community that is very different from those we are familiar with, although the moral choices of the characters are universal. The principal impetus here, though, is storytelling – and in that Jodi Picoult is skilled indeed.

JASON PINTER worked as an editor before becoming an author. He was commissioned to pen a series of novels in his Henry Parker series very quickly after having his first book published. That first novel was *The Mark* in 2007, with the young journo trying to prove himself innocent of the killing of a New York City police officer. The later *The Stolen* was named one of the best mysteries of 2008 by *Strand Magazine* and nominated for both the Shamus Award and the CrimeSpree Award for best paperback original.

Best known as creator of the cult TV series *True Detective*, **NIC PIZZOLATTO** is also a distinguished crime novelist (readers and viewers are generous enough not to lay the failure of the show's muddled second series at his door). Pizzolatto – of Italian lineage, as his name suggests – was born in New Orleans, Louisiana. After writing some well-received short stories, his first novel, *Galveston*, was published in 2010 to instant acclaim. In 2010, *Galveston* won the Prix du Premier Roman Étranger, the French Academy's award for best first novel from abroad, and it was also an Edgar Award finalist for best first novel.

RICHARD PRICE, born in the Bronx, New York City, wrote a notable first novel in his twenties with 1974's *The Wanderers*, a tough *bildungsroman* set in the Bronx in 1962/63. It was filmed in 1979 with a screenplay by Rose Kaufman and Philip Kaufman, who also directed. Price's signature book, though, is *Clockers*, which was nominated for the National Book Critics Circle Award and was filmed by Spike Lee; Price wrote the screenplay in collaboration with the director. The author's other screenplays include the Martin Scorsese adaption of Walter Tevis's *The Color of Money* (for which he was Oscar-nominated), 'Life Lessons' (the Scorsese segment of *New York Stories*) and 2000's updated take on *Shaft* with Samuel L Jackson. Like George Pelecanos, Price also wrote for the seminal HBO series *The Wire*. He won the Writers Guild of America Award for best dramatic series at the February 2008 ceremony for his work on the fifth season of *The Wire*.

Something of an American crime fiction institution, **BILL PRONZINI** has been remarkably consistent in his output over the years. His novel *Snowbound* received the Grand Prix de Littérature Policière as the best crime novel published in France in 1988. *A Wasteland of Strangers* was nominated for best crime novel of 1997 by both the Mystery Writers of America and the International Crime Writers' Association; in addition to six Edgar Award nominations, Pronzini has received three Shamus Awards, two for best novel, and the Lifetime Achievement Award. He lives in northern California with his wife, the crime novelist Marcia Muller.

MANUEL RAMOS's first novel, *The Ballad of Rocky Ruiz*, was a finalist for the Mystery Writers of America's Edgar Award. His books include *Desperado: A Mile High Noir*, which won the 2014 Colorado Book Award in the mystery category. *The Skull of Pancho Villa and Other Stories* appeared in 2015.

There's a possibly opportunistic echo in the writing of **CHRISTOPHER REICH** of Robert Ludlum's Bourne novels – or, to be more precise, the popular Matt Damon movies – but that's understandable in an overcrowded field, and Reich has the thriller-writing nous to deliver the goods. In *Rules of Vengeance*, Jonathan Ransom is holding down a job as a doctor in Kenya, while his wife has been obliged to go to ground, on the run from her previous employers. Ransom is now obliged to confront the consequences of his wife's duplicitous double life. This is kinetic fare, and it's nice to report that Reich has not forgotten the importance of character in big-scale thriller material such as this.

Are you irritated by the habit publishers have of trying to sell their new thriller writers by wildly inaccurate comparisons to more celebrated names in the genre? This strategy is employed in the (often vain) hope that we'll shell out for someone who's 'just as good as [fill in name] or your money back'. Fans of **KATHY REICHS** – and that's a great many readers – will be aware of her publishers likening her to the million-selling Patricia Cornwell, but for once the comparison is not over-optimistic; in fact, it's a tad redundant now.

A line that I once used in a newspaper review has found its way on to quite a few Reichs books, and I still stand by it: 'As each successive Reichs or Cornwell novel appears, it's becoming apparent that Reichs is not just "as good as" Cornwell, she has now become the finer writer.'

Kathy Reichs is eminently qualified to write the kind of detailed – and grisly – forensic crime novels that are her speciality. Born in Chicago, she was one of the few qualified forensic anthropologists to work in the US, dividing her duties between Quebec and the medical offices of the State of North Carolina. In her professional capacity, she has penned some definitive works in the forensics field, but for us non-specialists her defining book was her first novel, *Déjà Dead*, an authoritative thriller that instantly placed her at the top level in a very competitive field. This was the book that introduced Dr Temperance Brennan, a forensic anthropologist with virtually the same background as her creator (Reichs uses her expertise with impressive assurance). Brennan is the best of the many forensic specialists rubbing shoulders in the genre at present: she's cool (never, of course, given pause by her often grim profession), and always in charge of everything but her screwed-up private life. The equally impressive *Death du Jour* followed, while a later book, *Grave Secrets*, had Tempe travelling to a Guatemalan village, tracking the bodies of 23 women and children dumped in a mass grave. And it looked as if Reichs' winning streak was over, the change of locale fatally weakening her narrative grasp.

But when *Monday Mourning* appeared, admirers of Reichs and her feisty protagonist breathed a sigh of relief: all the cylinders were firing again – with just one thing preventing this one from being first-rank Reichs. Tempe is back on her old Montreal stamping ground, where she discovers the skeletons of three young girls in the basement of a pizza parlour. Colleagues (notably the caustic detective Luc Claudel) dismiss these as old bones, not for investigation. But Tempe is determined to prove that they are recent remains. Needless to say, her findings soon cut through the intransigence of her colleagues, and some dark secrets are pulled, kicking and screaming, into the light. The old Reichs tension is satisfyingly in evidence again, slightly undercut by the rather tired treatment of Tempe Brennan's messy, quixotic affair with detective Andrew Ryan – this is territory we know all too well, and there's nothing new here. But what makes this such a satisfying addition to the Reichs library (on a par with such winners as *Bare Bones* and *Fatal Voyage*) is the solid combination of a machine-tooled plot and the convincing picture of life at the sharp end in the world of forensic science. The skein of mystery and danger that Tempe encounters is created with skill, and the ever-accelerating unfolding of the plot has all the élan of Kathy Reichs at her most adroit.

The merest glance at the back catalogue of **JD ROBB** (better known as Nora Roberts) discloses one of the most prolific authors in the field, and while not everything has been top drawer in her imposing CV, her success rate is truly prodigious. *Obsession in Death* is among her best work. On a winter morning in New York, in a luxury apartment, the body of a woman lies dead on a massive bed. Scrawled in ink on the wall above her is a message: 'For Lieutenant Eve Dallas with great admiration and understanding.' For Dallas herself, celebrated for her high-profile cases, this is an unwelcome greeting – and tracking down her sinister admirer becomes a matter of urgency. We are back in ticking-clock territory, but those who've read other books by Roberts (under whatever name) will know that this is a secure area for the writer.

Not a great deal of nuance is to be found in the lengthy list of novels of **JAMES ROLLINS**, but a great deal of energy. The popular Sigma Force series includes *Sandstorm*, *Map of Bones*, *Black Order* and *The Judas Strain*. Not a million miles away from his customary action fare is his novelisation of Steven Spielberg's *Indiana Jones and the Kingdom of the Crystal Skull*. His Tucker Wayne series also has its advocates.

When I met **KAREN ROSE** at the Harrogate crime-writing festival, I was taken aback by the army of followers she had waiting to have books signed, quite as many as one might expect for writers better known in the UK. Rose is a bestselling novelist – in no uncertain terms. A characteristic book is *Have You Seen Her?* A serial killer has his sights set on cheerleaders in a small town in North Carolina. The girls, abducted from their beds, have something in common apart from their cheerleading duties – they each have long dark hair. It's imperative that the murderer is tracked down before he claims more victims, and Special Agent Steven Thatcher is dedicated to catching this monster. Thatcher is a widower and has his own problems: his son Brad is growing away from him. Brad's teacher, Jenna Marshall, is sympathetic, and a relationship grows between the detective and the teacher – but both Steven and Jenna are bruised and wary from earlier relationships. And the seemingly omniscient killer is setting traps – ever closer to his pursuer's home territory.

Rose first had success with her debut novel, 2003's *Don't Tell*. Her protagonist, Eve Wilson, is brutalised, left unconscious and requiring plastic surgery. And piling on the agony, Rose's subsequent book, *I Can See You*, subjected Eve to further agony. So it's something of a relief that *Have You Seen Her?* has different protagonists centre stage, even if they have to go through similar – though not quite as punishing – ordeals. Rose (who was a high school chemistry and physics teacher) knows how to maintain the tension.

SJ ROZAN (the initials conceal a female identity) has bagged the Edgar, Shamus, Anthony, Nero and Macavity Awards for best novel and the Edgar for best short story, and she has also received the Japanese Maltese Falcon Award. She has served on the national boards of Mystery Writers of America and Sisters in Crime, and is ex-president of the Private Eye Writers of America. She has written 11 books in her Lydia Chin and Bill Smith series. Also on her CV are standalone novels and numerous short stories. She runs a summer writing workshop in Assisi, Italy.

The talented San Francisco-born **GREG RUCKA** has a growing body of work as a novelist, with several books featuring bodyguard Atticus Kodiak and others focusing on Tara Chace, the protagonist of his Queen & Country series. He has excelled in the short story form and has brought a particular sophistication and finesse to the writing of comics. In the latter genre, apart from writing duties for Superman, he has found a parallel with his crime work by producing stories for Batman, the World's Greatest Detective.

MARCUS SAKEY's thrillers have been nominated for numerous awards, and his novel *Good People* was filmed with James Franco and Kate Hudson. Born in Michigan, Sakey attended that state's university before starting on a lengthy career in television and advertising, which (as he says) gave him 'plenty of exposure to liars and thieves'. His first crime novel, *The Blade Itself*, was sold at auction before publication. As research for his books, he has closely interacted with SWAT teams and bank robbers and even dissected a human brain. He now lives in Chicago.

Barry Forshaw

If you've been nurturing a particular writer at your bosom for years, secure and happy in the knowledge that he or she is known only to the cognoscenti, it's somewhat difficult to share your favourite when the whole world sits up and takes notice. That process started to happen for one of the very best writers in the crime fiction genre, **JAMES SALLIS**, after the film of his lean and sinewy masterpiece *Drive* opened (with Ryan Gosling as the protagonist). And if the first book that the new legion of Sallis fans picked up was *The Killer is Dying*, they would have quickly become aware of why the writer is held in such high esteem. The central character here is a hitman, committed to his final assignment; we are also introduced to a past-his-best detective with a mortally ill wife, and an abandoned boy living a nigh-feral existence on the streets. Around these three economically but trenchantly characterised protagonists, Sallis weaves his customary pared-down narrative, one that this time fruitfully combines several different strands of genre. Personally, I would be happy if James Sallis remained caviar to the general, but one cannot blame the writer and his publisher for wanting to achieve the kind of success that is available to many a less talented writer. And *The Killer is Dying* advanced the Sallis cause to considerable effect.

JOHN SANDFORD's series of 'Prey' novels has delivered flint-edged, precisely wrought thrillers that have never sacrificed character to the demands of a swiftly moving plot. That's certainly the case with *Naked Prey*, where the clammily realised north Minnesota setting is a major ingredient. Lucas Davenport is used to tricky assignments, and the one he undertakes for his old boss Rose, now a big wheel in law enforcement, is no exception. Two bodies have been found hanging from a tree – a white woman and a black man; an explosive combination that has the locals talking of lynching. Lucas isn't sure – and finds that some dark (and messy) secrets lie behind the deaths. The atmosphere conjured here is palpable, and the canvas that Sandford creates has an ambitiousness that English writers in the genre rarely aspire to.

All encomiums on book jackets from writers must be taken with a pinch of salt (and I include my own), but in the case of **LISA**

SCOTTOLINE they are fully justified. In such books as *Moment of Truth* and *Mistaken Identity*, Scottoline has shown that she is a writer of real imagination and skill, often complementing the pulse-racing excitement of her novels with a nice line in sardonic humour. There is less of that humour in the nightmare tale that is *Courting Trouble*: Anne Murphy is a lawyer preparing herself for her role as defence in an important trial. But the Fourth of July celebrations in Philadelphia are a distraction, and she retires to a secluded beach house in order to work. Her idyll is rudely interrupted when she sees a front-page headline in the morning paper announcing that she has been savagely killed. Anne finds that the police are unable to track down the stalker who is on her tail, and she decides to continue to play dead in order to survive. And as the danger grows ever nearer, she has to rely on the all-female law firm of Rosato and Associates to help her track down and confront a brutal murderer. The beleaguered heroine is something of a cliché these days, but Scottoline manages to invest Anne with a strongly defined personality and the reader is quickly involved in her dangerous situation. This is a truly dynamic piece of work – and one is even prepared to swallow the rather unlikely all-female team of lawyers.

JAMES SHEEHAN produces unspectacular but efficient work with such books as *The Law of Second Chances*. For 17 years, Henry Wilson has cooled his heels on death row for a crime he is innocent of – but death by lethal injection is looming in eight weeks. Benny Avrile is a petty criminal, pursued by the police for his part in a violent robbery. The destiny of both men will be affected by canny trial lawyer Jack Tobin. High-octane legal thriller fare, delivered with real energy.

JAMES SIEGEL's *Derailed* is typical Siegel fare. He works from a sure-fire premise: the ordinary man torn from a boring, quotidian existence and plunged into a nightmare. This scenario has served many artists well (think John Buchan's *The Thirty-Nine Steps* or Hitchcock's *North by Northwest*), but this is one of the most assured treatments of the theme. Charles Schine is on his way to work, conscious that his life moves along well-oiled tracks. But then he encounters the beautiful and enigmatic Lucinda Harris, and his association with her not only pulls apart the well-ordered fabric of his day-to-day routine but threatens his very life. Charles has to learn – very quickly – some basic survival tactics, not to mention the niceties of dealing with some very dangerous people. And it's in the latter area that Siegel really shines: his villains, from petty thugs to more urbane and dangerous *éminences grises*, are drawn with a very varied and imaginative skill, with street language rendered quite as plausibly as the exchanges involving top-level corruption. The first-person narrative works well in terms of involving the reader.

JEFFREY SIGER is an American author who writes the Inspector Kaldis series set in Greece. His debut was a bestselling English-language book in Greece, and (as of 2016) there are now eight titles in the series. He has been nominated for a Barry Award and has been chair of the Bouchercon festival. The Greek settings of his novels are vividly realised.

Choose an author as you choose a friend, said Lord Roscommon. But such strictures would hardly apply if the author were **KARIN SLAUGHTER**. No doubt Ms Slaughter is kind to her relatives and strokes small animals in the street, but her books? Anything but friendly. In fact, the creator of such books as *Blindsighted* and *Kisscut* is comfortably ahead of the pack in the art of flesh-creeping. What's more, she clearly regards each new book as a challenge in terms of inducing reader terror, as books such as *Broken* prove. We're back in the company of former Grant County medical examiner Sara Linton, up to her elbows in blood, *comme d'habitude*. A woman's body is found in the waters of Lake Grant, and a note discovered nearby suggests that the death is a suicide – but Sara quickly decides it isn't. The prime suspect in the murder makes a frantic plea to see Sara – but when she arrives at his cell in the local police station, she is confronted with grim news: Tommy Braham, whom she'd known as a little boy, is dead. He has been badly beaten, and both of his wrists are slashed open. On the wall, written in his blood, are the words 'Not me'. Sara grows suspicious of the detective in charge of the case, Lena Adams, and contacts the Georgia Bureau of Investigation.

Special Agent Will Trent finds his vacation cut short in order to aid Sara – but both of them find that a vicious killer is protected by an implacable wall of non-cooperation that the cloistered community of Grant County has built around itself.

In fact, Slaughter's work is a high-pressure reworking of the Southern Gothic strain, and like so many of her illustrious predecessors, she knows precisely how to take the reader into the darker corners of the human psyche – and it's not a comfortable place to be. Her vividly created locale, Heartsdale, in Grant County, is matched by her solidly drawn protagonists, Chief of Police Jeffrey Tolliver and his ex-wife Sara Linton (the town's medical examiner and paediatrician). The autopsy in *Kisscut* brought to light a gallery of horrors, and a later book, *Indelible*, is similarly unsuitable for squeamish readers. Sara and Tolliver are taking a break from their professional lives to work on their tricky relationship, and a weekend at the beach seems like a good idea. But a detour to Jeffrey's home town proves to be a bad move: his friend Robert shoots an assailant who has broken into his house. Jeffrey takes his friend's side in the matter, but there are grey areas for Sara. There's Robert's distressed wife, Jessie, who doesn't seem to echo her husband's story. And when it looks like Jeffrey has made some alterations to the crime scene, not only is his relationship with Sara under strain, but a savage killer may be able to carry on his bloody work unobstructed – with Jeffrey and Sara as targets.

Slaughter is now routinely compared to Thomas Harris, and the comparisons are not far-fetched. We're used to unflinching forensic detail these days, courtesy of such writers as Kathy Reichs and Patricia Cornwell, but Slaughter is adept at unsettling the reader in a whole host of ways, not least her recurrent suggestion that the patina of normality that sustains her characters is very thin indeed. Tolliver and Sara's faltering relationship is richly drawn, but the reduced attention given to their private problems as the novel progresses is complemented by the author's polished and consummate handling of the tortuous plot.

In the UK at the end of the last millennium, a certain reaction against notably violent female writers such as Slaughter and Tess Gerritsen built up a head of steam, and her books provided ammunition for those who prefer crime fiction that leaves the reader stirred but not shaken. Those of us not hindered by such compunctions can safely negotiate the unsettling Slaughter universe with the comforting knowledge that pulse rates will be pleasurably accelerated. But there's more to this writer than the mayhem her surname suggests – her own upbringing in a small South Georgia town is something Slaughter frequently parlays into multifaceted, highly persuasive portraits of a community not at ease with itself. She may not be an author you choose as a friend, but she's still bloody good company.

Having produced one of the great twentieth-century crime novels in the remarkable *Gorky Park*, **MARTIN CRUZ SMITH** has taken his sleuth Renko through the years up to the modern era. *Three Stations* focuses on an industry that the Russians are none too proud of: sex tourism. On a train heading from Moscow, the teenage Maya and her newly born daughter travel in an insalubrious carriage where family squabbles and clandestine sex take place around them. Rescued from a drunken soldier, Maya thinks she has found a friend in the elderly Lena. But Maya is drugged and wakes up to find all her possessions gone – along with her baby. Lena is nowhere to be seen. At the same time, Renko is summoned to the eponymous Three Stations, where the body of a woman, possibly a prostitute, has been found. Peerless stuff. The real achievement of *Three Stations* lies in two elements: firstly, the conflicted Arkady Renko, who will never take no for an answer, whatever the consequences; and secondly, the author's pungent evocation of modern Russia – in all its vitality and corruption.

Desperation Road is an outstanding literary novel that bodes well for the career of the writer **MICHAEL FARRIS SMITH**. A dark but ultimately redemptive tale, this is a major breakout novel from one of the most promising writers of his generation. The author's subsequent novel, *The Fighter* (not yet published at the time of writing), is already building a head of steam in anticipation after the well-received earlier book.

ALEXANDRA SOKOLOFF is a familiar face on the UK side of the Atlantic nowadays, as she splits her time between California and Scotland. She has produced a variety of thrillers (some paranormal, some pure crime), after a career move from screenwriting. Sokoloff has won an International Thriller Writers Award, and has been nominated for an Anthony Award and a Bram Stoker Award.

A palpable sense of danger haunts **PETER SPIEGELMAN**'s *Black Maps*, and that pleasurable unsettling of the reader is a constant factor. Spiegelman's shop-worn hero, private eye John March, is struggling to pull himself together after the misfortunes that have blighted both his life and his career. Manhattan is his beat, but when a Park Avenue client employs him, he becomes involved in a case that has a million ramifications – most of them dangerous. Rick Pierro, March's client, is a self-made man who has transcended his low-rent origins to become a star performer on Wall Street. But everything that Rick has acquired – including his desirable wife – is on the line when an unwelcome communication threatens to pull him into a massive financial scandal. John March tracks down a ferociously intelligent opponent who has left banks and people bleeding in his wake, and he discovers that layers of corruption run very deep indeed. It's no longer a novelty for a thriller writer to have a financial background, but there's no denying that Spiegelman uses his knowledge more impressively than most, and the result is a highly involving piece of work.

Don't look for heroes in Spiegelman's *Thick as Thieves* – you won't find any. The sinister world of criminal 'black money' and the clandestine laundering carried out at law-proof banking havens around the world (where no questions are ever asked about the shadowy clients) are at the centre of the author's involving crime novel. But this is not a part of the series featuring the author's recurring private investigator John March – the central characters here are thieves (there are no real 'good guys'), and if the reader feels guilty rooting for the protagonists' ingenious grand larceny, there is some compensation afforded by the fact that the anti-heroes of *Thick as Thieves* are a step higher up the moral ladder than the nasty individuals they are attempting to shake down.

CIA agent Carr makes a dishonest living by planning robberies in Houston, and is commissioned by another criminal to forge an elite team of highly professional thieves. Carr is persuaded (against his better judgement) to take the job of separating a disgraced financier, Curtis Prager, from his millions of dollars. Prager has been lucky so far, evading justice over money-laundering and conspiracy accusations (the key witnesses being lined up to testify against him have all died) and he is consolidating his fortune offering financial advice to top-drawer mobsters in the Caymans. The task for Carr and his team is to crack Prager's complex security arrangements, and it is a massively dangerous operation – the level of risk ratcheted up by the fact that one of Carr's colleagues (a woman with whom he is having an affair) may not be all that she seems. But neither is Carr…

This is an ace thriller – wonderfully tense stuff delivered with the foot-to-the-pedal panache that Spiegelman has previously shown in such books as the award-winning *Black Maps* discussed above.

ERICA SPINDLER has long been one of the most reliable of bestselling authors, and such books as *The First Wife* deliver everything that readers have come to expect. Her female protagonist, Bailey Browne, is in love with the attractive Logan, and she is unworried by the ten-year age gap between the couple. Similarly, their backgrounds are very different – he is immensely rich. But when he brings Bailey home to his impressive estate on 90 wooded acres, things very quickly begin to go wrong. She hears rumours about what happened to Logan's first wife, and then a local woman disappears; circumstances suggest that it is Bailey's new husband who is behind the disappearance. Has she made a massive mistake in this relationship? The theme of women finding that their marriages are not all they seem to be is at the centre of a great deal of current crime fiction, but Spindler delivers a riff on the shop-worn notion.

In *Breakneck*, Detective MC Riggio is on the point of getting married. The age of 30 is just around the corner, and she finally feels that her life and career are going the way she wants them to. But then her cousin Tommy is killed, and suddenly everything for her is new and disturbing. There is a ruthless, emotion-free serial killer, the eponymous Breakneck, plying a hideous trade; and it's up to MC to channel her sorrow and anger in a positive way to track down a monster – before others die. *Breakneck* features two strong heroines – Riggio and her partner, Kitt Lundgren – who first appeared in the earlier *Copycat*.

DANA STABENOW was raised on a 75-foot fish tender in the Gulf of Alaska, and after receiving a BA in journalism from the University of Alaska, she worked (profitably) for such companies as BP. Her first Kate Shugak novel, *A Cold Day for Murder*, was published in 1992 and won an Edgar Award. She has been adding to her roster of novels featuring Star Svensdotter (which are science fiction) and Liam Campbell (about an Alaska state trooper), alongside those with her signature character Kate Shugak – the tally for the latter now over 20.

As his adroit psychological thriller *Hard Feelings* comprehensively demonstrated, **JASON STARR** is a writer with a uniquely penetrating style and a satirical streak, and the later *Tough Luck* has all the impressive marshalling of character, plot and action that marks his best work. Mickey Prada works in a neighbourhood seafood market in Brooklyn putting fish on ice. He has delayed college a year to help his sick dad. But Mickey's got a problem. He's made some unfortunate friends, and his bookie is after him. So when his best friend, Chris, asks Mickey to join him on a can't-lose caper, Mickey decides to go along. But, sure-fire schemes often have a way of backfiring, and this one is sending Mickey into an uncharted part of Brooklyn, where catastrophe awaits. A sharp, edgy and stylishly written noir thriller.

His UK success, inaugurated in 1997 with his first crime novel, *Cold Caller*, instantly established him as a distinctive voice on the crime scene; his second, *Nothing Personal*, which concerned a compulsive gambler who comes up with a kidnapping scheme to settle his debts, was another powerfully persuasive book. Starr has been a leading proponent and author of the dark domestic thriller for almost 20 years and is one of only a handful of writers to have won the Anthony Award for mystery fiction multiple times. Starr also writes screenplays, has had several plays performed by off-off Broadway theatre companies in New York, and produces inventive scripts for comics. When queried as to why (up until *The Pack*) he penned standalone novels and hadn't created a series character, he replied: 'New York City is my series character.'

CHARLIE STELLA was born in Manhattan and raised in Brooklyn. His introduction to crime fiction was via a reading of George V Higgins' *The Friends of Eddie Coyle*, which opened up the possibilities of the genre to him. Such novels as Stella's *Johnny Porno* have made a mark. Set in New York City in 1973, Stella's vibrant seventh crime novel deals with the quotidian life of low-rent organised crime types, with influences from Elmore Leonard and (of course) George V Higgins.

TAYLOR STEVENS' *The Doll* features Vanessa 'Michael' Munroe, an information specialist with a worldwide reputation for getting results – and usually risking personal danger in order to do so. But her confrontational style has led to her acquiring a variety of dangerous enemies. She is kidnapped and taken to a dark underground world in which women are bought and sold, where she is at the disposal of a sinister controller: the Doll Maker. Other writers such as Lee Child have praised Vanessa Munroe as a distinctive new character, and the storytelling ethos here is absolutely spot-on.

JOHN STRALEY chose – reluctantly – to live in the wilds of Alaska, and has never looked back. The Shamus Award-winning author of *The Curious Eat Themselves* and *The Woman Who Married a Bear* was appointed the Writer Laureate of Alaska in 2006. Straley worked for years in Sitka as a criminal defence investigator, and his literary work has an identity quite unlike that of his contemporaries.

WALLACE STROBY is both an award-winning journalist and the author of a variety of accomplished novels, four of which feature professional thief Crissa Stone. A lifelong resident of the Jersey Shore, his first novel, *The Barbed-Wire Kiss*, boasted an acute sense of place (a vividly described New Jersey) and was a finalist for the 2004 Barry Award for best first novel.

Don't be put off by the title of **PETER SWANSON**'s *The Girl with a Clock for a Heart*, which suggests a catchpenny grab for the Stieg Larsson market; this is a distinctive and involving thriller that is nothing at all like the work of the late Swedish writer. In a Boston bar, business manager George Foss spots Liana, a girlfriend from college whom he hasn't seen for 20 years. His involvement back then left him with romantic scars and a part in a murder investigation. But George's old girlfriend is to lead him into new, far worse, trouble. She is on the run, and inveigles the hapless George into acting as a courier to return $500,000 that she took from a former lover. What's more, there is a ruthless thug on her trail. Unsurprisingly, everything goes disastrously wrong – as anyone who's seen such yuppies-in-peril films as *Something Wild* will have anticipated. The book has two time lines, one dealing with the love affair in the past between Liana and George, and the more dangerous present; both sections are handled with authority, but the present-day segments are inevitably more compelling. Liana is a touch underdeveloped as a character, but the labyrinthine plot here has a grip of high-tensile steel.

Of course, each new debut crime novel arrives with lashings of unpersuasive hyperbole from the publisher, but sometimes it's justified. That was certainly the case with Swanson's first book, but many a tyro writer falls at the hurdle of the second book: did Swanson's *The Kind Worth Killing* break this disappointing progression? At a London airport, Ted Severson bonds with a woman he meets over cocktails and they concoct an outrageous criminal plan – but do both of them mean to go through with it? This central premise may be borrowed from *Strangers on a Train*, but Swanson takes the notion in some truly startling directions, excelling in the vividly etched characterisation of his protagonists (such as Ted's ruthless wife Miranda, nurturing her own secrets). But what makes *The Kind Worth Killing* so enjoyable is the beautifully constructed plotting – leaving aside all the book's other virtues, that element alone comfortably sees off 'second novel syndrome'.

DUANE SWIERCZYNSKI is the Edgar-nominated author of several noteworthy novels, including *Canary* and *Severance Package* and the Shamus Award-winning Charlie Hardie series (*Fun and Games*, *Hell* *and Gone, Point and Shoot*). Comics are also a speciality, with 250-plus outings for Marvel, DC and others under his belt. Swierczynski has also collaborated with *CSI* creator Anthony E Zuiker on the Level 26 series.

The prolific **BRAD THOR**'s hefty catalogue numbers 15 titles (so far) featuring ex-Navy SEAL Secret Service agent Scot Harvath, including *Code of Conduct, Act of War, Black List, Foreign Influence* (the latter notably well reviewed) and *The Last Patriot* (which was nominated best thriller of the year by the International Thriller Writers association). Other work includes the standalone *The Athena Project*, though this too may become the first in a sequence. Productivity is Thor's name of the game.

PJ TRACY is the pseudonym of mother-daughter writing duo PJ and Traci Lambrecht, winners of the Anthony, Barry, Gumshoe and Minnesota Book Awards. Their first three novels, *Monkeewrench, Live Bait* and *Dead Run*, became national and international bestsellers, success later consolidated by *Shoot to Thrill* and *Two Evils.*
  When I met 'PJ Tracy', I found that (rather like the male and female components of 'Nicci French') they do not divide their writing duties along the lines one might expect; just as Sean French and Nicci Gerrard swap male and female characters, PJ and Traci do not exclusively deal with characters from their own generations – the reverse, in fact. This clearly is a winning strategy, as *Two Evils* comprehensively proves.
  A young girl is found in a parking lot with her throat cut. Shortly afterwards, the police discover the bodies of two youthful immigrants in a seedy apartment. The body count continues to rise. Homicide detectives Gino Rolseth and Leo Magozzi of the Minneapolis Police Department suspect that these killings are not random, but they can make no connections. They turn to computer whiz Grace MacBride for assistance – a move that puts her in the direst danger. Before long, the two detectives, at their wits' end, find themselves having to confront the eponymous 'Two Evils'... and possibly die trying.
  All of the elements that made the previous books under the

Tracy banner so successful are in evidence here, including the pithy interplay between Rolseth and Magozzi and their own personal Lisbeth Salander, computer maven Grace MacBride. But sharply characterised though the trio are, there are other things that distinguish *Two Evils*: plotting of immense ingenuity and the authors' gift for genuinely speakable, sardonic dialogue (the latter a rarer skill than you might imagine in the crime and thriller field).

Sadly, as this book was going to print, I learned of Patricia 'PJ' Lambrecht's death. Her daughter, however, has said that she will continue the writing name solo.

Are sequels to successful novels really a good idea? Shakespeare ensured that there would be no further appearances for Lear and Hamlet, but there are different imperatives in the popular arts – and it might be argued that Sherlock Holmes and 007 were more engaging characters before their creators trotted them out once too often. So was **SCOTT TUROW** wise to bring back the hero of his groundbreaking novel, *Presumed Innocent*, over 20 years after that book inaugurated the legal thriller as a cash-cow genre?

Presumed Innocent was a blueprint for the field, with a fascinating mass of legal detail giving weight to its plausibility. The book is narrated by Rusty Sabich, a married prosecuting attorney. After his ex-lover Carolyn is murdered, Sabich finds himself accused of the murder, but the real killer is close to home. It is a terrific book, but by penning a sequel 23 years later, Turow has made himself something of a hostage to fortune.

In *Innocent*, Rusty is now 60 and a senior appeal court judge. He finds himself once again accused of murder – his disturbed wife Barbara is the victim. His old nemesis, detective Tommy Molto, is now a prosecuting attorney and rubbing his hands at the prospect of finally putting his quarry behind bars. The most incriminating circumstances involve the fact that Rusty woke up to find his wife dead at his side but waited – without apparent reason – for a full day before notifying anyone. What killed her was an overdose of drugs, and Rusty had recently dealt with a case in which the same antidepressants were used. What is the reason behind his damning silence?

This is a pre-sold novel, such is the hold that its illustrious predecessor has on the popular imagination. And it's refreshing to report that Turow's narrative skills have not deserted him; he remains a consummate storyteller. He needs to be, as in this book Turow asks the reader to accept some fairly mind-boggling suppositions, such as the unlikely survival of the Sabich marriage after the events of the first book. So – was a sequel a good idea? While *Innocent* is not in the league of the earlier book, it's still an immensely professional piece of work, with a particularly acute grasp of the psychology of its various characters; it also provides a useful series of pointers on how not to behave if accused of spousal murder.

Thinking of sampling the work of **LISA UNGER**? Nicely representative is *Black Out*. Living in an upscale Florida suburb, Annie Powers' life appears to be highly satisfactory, with a loving husband and a beautiful daughter. But fissures begin to appear in her idyllic lifestyle when dark events of the past come back to plague her – events that she has no recollection of. As in the bestselling *Beautiful Lies*, Lisa Unger once again proves that she is highly adroit at the psychological thriller.

Known for his commitment to social issues, the New York writer **ANDREW VACHSS** works in multiple disciplines: crime fiction novelist, child protection consultant, and attorney exclusively representing children and youths. He also serves as a law guardian in New York State. Vachss has written over 30 novels and several collections of short stories, along with work as a poet, playwright, lyricist and writer of graphic novels. His Burke series of hard-boiled novels may be his best-known work; that series concluded with *Another Life* in 2008.

After completing the Burke sequence, Vachss started two new series. The first book in the Dell and Dolly trilogy was *Aftershock*, in 2013, with the second novel, *Shockwave*, a year later. The Cross series incorporates supernatural elements to address Vachss' concern about the vulnerability of children. Vachss is a member of PEN and the Writers Guild of America.

An Honorable Man is a striking debut novel by talented US writer **PAUL VIDICH**. Written in the style of Alan Furst and John le Carré (but retaining a distinct individual character), it is a tense Cold War thriller set in 1950s Washington DC. Vidich's subsequent novel, *The Good Assassin*, received an enthusiastic response and much interest from non-US publishers.

JOSEPH WAMBAUGH shook the American police novel free of its clichés to produce something gritty, truthful, authentic – and notably unvarnished. His first four books and his stint on the *Police Story* television series in the 1970s have proved to be seminal. The son of a policeman (key to his background as a writer), Wambaugh became an LAPD cop himself, subsequently receiving a master's degree in 1968 while working as a detective sergeant at Hollenbeck Station in the barrio of Los Angeles. He continued to work as a policeman even when success as a novelist arrived. *The Choirboys* (filmed by hardnosed director Robert Aldrich) is probably the Wambaugh key book, although *The Onion Field* is also important.

American author **JASON WEBSTER** (who lives in Spain) has written several compelling non-fiction books about his adopted country. Among his crime fiction, *Or the Bull Kills You*, featuring his canny copper Max Cámara, is a particularly zesty offering. Max is not a fan of bull fighting, but finds himself obliged to judge a festival *corrida* with Spain's most celebrated young matador. But that night, back in the ring, he finds something particularly horrible that leads him into one of his strangest and most disturbing cases. Webster told me that evoking a strong sense of place is important for him – and it's an accomplishment he has firmly under his belt.

STEPHEN WHITE's swift-paced *Warning Signs* joined such books as *Harm's Way* and *Higher Authority* as evidence of his skill. In a pool of blood and shattered pottery, the body of Royal Peterson, controversial district attorney for Boulder County, is discovered. To her dismay, crack homicide detective Lucy Tanner finds that she is the prime suspect in a case that is already having massive political repercussions for a nervous city. As Lucy struggles to find out who has beaten Peterson to death while his bedridden wife slept upstairs, clinical psychologist Alan Gregory is one of the few who finds it hard to accept that Lucy is responsible, and (along with his wife Lauren, prosecutor in the dead man's office) he decides to defend the beleaguered Lucy Tanner. The description 'psychological thriller' is overused these days, and many authors have only the most tenuous grasp on the psychology of the characters. Not so Mr White, who delivers trenchant psychological portraits of all of his very different protagonists, notably the up-against-the-wall Lucy Tanner. White's Alan Gregory novels have made his name familiar, drawing on over 15 years of clinical practice as a psychologist to render persuasive and plausible characters. White grew up in New York, New Jersey and Southern California and received his PhD in clinical psychology from the University of Colorado in 1979, after which he became known as an authority on the psychological effects of marital disruption, especially on men. His acquaintanceship with a colleague in Los Angeles, another paediatric psychologist named Jonathan Kellerman, had repercussions; both men are now successful crime novelists

If you haven't heard of **DON WINSLOW**, don't worry – it's not a cause for shame. But if you *have* heard of him – and you have now – you've joined a coterie of people who know the name of a very special talent. This laconic New York-born writer is regarded by the *au courant* as one of the best in the field; his sprawling, visceral drug crime novel *The Power of the Dog* rivalled the Grand Master of that genre, Robert Stone. Opinion is more divided over later books set in California's surfer territory, in which Winslow has tried (and sometimes succeeded) to suggest that this laid-back community is in possession of more than a single brain cell. But did admirers' pleas for a return to the massive reach of *The Power of the Dog* result in the novel *Savages*? Violent drug-dealing conflict is back, but now shot through with the mordant humour of his recent surfing novels; the result is quite splendid.

Despite Ben's apparent environmental concerns, he's more than ready to handle big-time marijuana deals with his ex-mercenary friend Chon in Laguna Beach. Chon is the muscle, securing their territory against incursions, and they share a girlfriend, an Orange County beauty called Ophelia. It goes without saying that everything turns sour. A video arrives, with shots of severed heads suggesting that there will be bloody consequences when the Baja cartel moves in. Ophelia is snatched, and Ben and Chon are instructed to hand over the business. It's obvious they don't stand a chance going up against such a ruthless nemesis. But guess whether or not they decide to try?

Winslow is not concerned with keeping his readers in a comfortable place, and the challenges begin by making us complicit with his less-than-admirable dope-dealing anti-heroes. The badinage of the beleaguered protagonists – one a laid-back save-the-planet type, the other a tough ex-SEAL, and between them a ragbag of SoCal attitudes – is wonderfully funny, but there's also a slew of acidic socio-political commentaries on American society, and some nifty wordplay; Winslow has few equals in the latter area.

Film studios are snapping at the author's heels. Oliver Stone filmed *Savages*, but with limited success. Stone, whose style as a director is like a blow to the solar plexus, has never been noted for nuance (he gave frictionless, comfortable rides to such politicians as Hugo Chávez in *South of the Border*); Don Winslow, however, is a writer for whom nuance and multiple levels are articles of faith. But Winslow clearly didn't stand behind Oliver Stone with a revolver, as Werner Herzog used to do when filming with Klaus Kinski.

Don Winslow was born in New York City but raised on Rhode Island. He has done many things on his way to being a novelist: during apartheid, he smuggled money to help raise funds to build schools in Soweto, worked as a safari guide in Kenya, had a stint in the mountains of western China, and simulated hostage exchanges while working as a 'mock' terrorist for the Institute for International Studies. He has also worked in the theatre and film, as a private investigator, and as an independent consultant to law firms on issues involving litigation arising from criminal behaviour. His first novel, *A Cool Breeze on the Underground* – which is mostly set in London – was nominated for the Edgar Award, and a later book, *California Fire and Life*, received the Shamus Award. A feature film of his *The Death and Life of Bobby Z* came out in 2007, starring Paul Walker and Laurence Fishburne.

DANIEL WOODRELL's distinctive novels and short stories are mostly set in the Ozarks in Missouri. The author himself described his work as 'Country Noir'; he was referring specifically to his novel *Give Us a Kiss*, but the phrase has stuck as a generic term for Woodrell's books. Those who have read his work (and that's a growing number of admirers) will know that he absolutely defies categorisation, and that's very much the case with *Winter's Bone*, his calling card book (successfully filmed by Debra Granik). This tale of love and endurance in an unforgiving American Midwest is memorable indeed, with the heroine, Ree, forced to look after her sedated mother. But she soon has more pressing – and violent – problems. Powerful and unusual, with a strongly etched sense of its frigid locale.

The writer **STUART WOODS** hails from Manchester, Georgia and graduated from the University of Georgia with a BA in sociology. At the end of the 1960s, he moved to London and worked there for three years in various advertising agencies. In early 1973, he decided to become a novelist. *Chiefs* in 1981 made his name; the book won the Edgar Allan Poe prize from the Mystery Writers of America, and Woods was later nominated again for *Palindrome*. He has also been awarded France's Grand Prix de Littérature Policière for *Imperfect Strangers*.

The jacket of *Dark Origins* credits **ANTHONY E ZUIKER** as the creator of *CSI*, and with one of the most acclaimed of TV crime series under his belt, expectations were high for Zuiker as a novelist. *Dark Origins* (co-written with Duane Swierczynski) – largely speaking – fulfilled those expectations. A psychopath called Sqweegel has killed over 35 people over three decades. Only one individual has ever got close to catching this monster, and Steve Dark is no longer interested in tracking down such individuals. But Sqweegel (who also sports a nasty line in torture, along with his pleasure in murder) is at his customary pursuits, and those on his trail this time belong to a clandestine unit called Level 26. They're not doing too well, with their professional reputations – and their lives – under threat. They must persuade the recalcitrant Steve Dark to exercise his old skills. Complemented by a sophisticated online and digital element, including film content, this is chilling and authoritative.

... and (courtesy of J Kingston Pierce of The Rap Sheet*), a selection of US crime authors not discussed above who are also worthy of attention:*

Julia Dahl, Ivy Pochoda, Gar Anthony Haywood, Andrew Hunt, Robin Burcell, Michael Harvey, Lou Berney, Anthony Neil Smith, Todd Robinson, Dave Zeltserman, Ronald Tierney, Ingrid Thoft, Eric Beetner, Alan Russell, Lee Goldberg, Tod Goldberg, Patricia Abbott, Daniel Silva, Lisa Brackmann, Chris Knopf, Laura McHugh, Dick Lochte, Benjamin Whitmer, Robert Dugoni, William Lashner, Bill Loehfelm and Rachel Howzell Hall.

3: Selected Crime Films
and TV of the New Millennium

The approach adopted here is to cover dramas made in the twenty-first century, but I include shows that began in the last millennium and continued into this one, such as NYPD Blue.

BAD LIEUTENANT (film, 2009)

Abel Ferrara's original 1992 cult film – with its bitter and caustic picture of a self-loathing corrupt cop played by Harvey Keitel – was always going to be a hard act to follow for any remake, and it took a certain chutzpah from the German arthouse director Werner Herzog (of all directors) to take another stab at the same scenario. With the reliable Nicolas Cage in the title role in the film (subtitled *Port of Call: New Orleans*), Herzog found another provocative approach to the material, with Cage meeting the challenge and giving a performance that almost matched Keitel's in intensity. Herzog claimed never to have seen the original and the more blackly comic tone of this version suggested he might have been telling the truth.

BIG APPLE (TV, 2001)

Despite its brief life, *Big Apple* sported some modest virtues – unsurprising, given that it was the brainchild of the talented David Milch, responsible for the influential *NYPD Blue*. Directors of the series were generally encouraged to bring a nervy, kinetic approach to their work, and Ed O'Neill put in particularly commendable work as a police officer with a variety of personal and professional conflicts.

BOARDWALK EMPIRE (TV, 2010–14)

The improvisatory quality of the pilot episode of *Boardwalk Empire* was not to be replicated in the rest of the series. The reason? Martin Scorsese – who favours the extempore method in his work – was contracted to direct this opening segment (a canny commercial move, much used in the promotion of the series), but subsequent directors largely eschewed this approach, long something of a shibboleth in TV production. Set in the Prohibition era of the 1920s, the show's central character is Enoch 'Nucky' Thompson, the Machiavellian treasurer of Atlantic City in New Jersey. Moving easily between gangsters and politicians, Nucky (a typically distinctive performance by Steve Buscemi) plays both ends against the middle in ruthless fashion. But then he draws the unwelcome attention of the federal government, which has started to take an interest in his conspicuously upscale mode of living. The show was well received and showcased some excellent performers (such as Michael Shannon) but never quite fulfilled the promise of the send-off Scorsese granted it.

BONES (TV, 2005–)
The Temperance Brennan books of Kathy Reichs did not lend themselves easily to TV adaptation, which no doubt accounts for the radical finessing they received in this series. A wise move in the event, given that the show was a palpable hit. *Bones* adopted a less astringent tone than many of its rivals, and won viewers' affection – as attested by the fact that it has accrued a respectable 11 seasons and 250-plus episodes so far. The show, though, remains essentially a snapshot of Kathy Reichs' novels.

BOSCH (TV, 2014–)
More than most literary coppers, readers appear to have myriad mental visions of Michael Connelly's dogged cop Hieronymus 'Harry' Bosch, and it is a measure of the achievement of the actor Titus Welliver, along with the creative personnel behind this TV series (such as showrunner Eric Ellis Overmyer), that the approval level for the show was so high. Inevitably, the complexity of the novels is slightly smoothed out, but quite a large degree of the world that Connelly created for his forceful detective finds its way – somewhat refracted – into the show.

BREAKING BAD/BETTER CALL SAUL (TV, 2008–13, 2015–)

The curious cultural phenomenon that quickly attached itself to the Danish drama *The Killing* – the necessity on the part of many people to apologise for not having seen the show after it became *de rigueur* viewing – was also notable with Vince Gilligan's remarkable, groundbreaking series. But those who made excuses rather than actually viewing the show did themselves a disservice. Perhaps even more than in the case of *The Sopranos* (discussed below), *Breaking Bad* quickly established itself as the quintessential example of long-form television, in which the texture, complexity and character development typical of a novel were injected into a televisual format. As we follow the cancer-afflicted chemistry teacher Walter White's ever more horrendous progression into a world of drugs and crime, there is an echo of Robert Warshow's essay 'The Gangster as Tragic Hero', with Walter moving from maladroit amateur drug manufacturer to monstrous inhuman killer and ruthless drug lord. The multifaceted character is brilliantly incarnated in Bryan Cranston's layered performance. That series' slippery, fast-talking criminal lawyer played by Bob Odenkirk was moved centre stage in the enjoyable follow-up *Better Call Saul*; more mordantly comic in tone but still catnip for admirers of the original series.

CASTLE (TV, 2009–16)

A highly successful crime show with (as protagonist) a crime novelist, Rick Castle, who works with a tough female New York cop, who acts as inspiration for his writing work. The show lasted eight seasons and ran to over 170 episodes before shutting up shop in 2016. A particularly ingratiating – and not too self-conscious – touch was the notion of guest spots in the show by real-life crime writers, notably Michael Connelly, Dennis Lehane, James Patterson and Stephen Cannell. The show also led to several serviceable tie-in novels.

THE CLOSER (TV, 2005–12)

Not always rising above the generic, this is a show that nevertheless found some new wrinkles in the crime genre, and its eight-year run demonstrated that it was doing something right. The show reflects the British show *Prime Suspect* with its beleaguered female copper (played by Kyra Sedgwick) encountering hostile males in the police department – some even requesting transfers before they've even met her. Sedgwick's character is also reminiscent of Lynda La Plante's Jane Tennison in another respect, with the detective's messy personal life and casual attitude to her own health.

COLD CASE (TV, 2003–10)

If TV re-runs are an index of popularity (and they are), this much-seen, much-circulated show is a winner, although it was finally decommissioned in 2010. The characters are the members of a Philadelphia-based crew of detectives working on the eponymous 'cold cases' as new evidence appears. Frequently by-the-numbers, but with virtues.

COLLATERAL (film, 2004)

A demonstration of Tom Cruise's oft-maligned thespian skills was this taut Michael Mann thriller, in which the star acquits himself well as the ice-cold hitman who hijacks a taxi and its hapless driver (the latter played by Jamie Foxx). Cruise has played against type several times, and he is particularly effective here, with Mann's customary visual stylishness highlighted by the fact that the film was shot on both film and digital video.

CRIMINAL MINDS (TV, 2005–)

With the criminal profilers of the FBI's Behavioral Analysis Unit as protagonists, this highly successful show has run to 11 seasons and more than 250 episodes. At the time of writing, the series has been renewed for a twelfth season. There have been two spin-offs, the brief run of *Criminal Minds: Suspect Behavior* (which ran for just one season in 2011) and *Criminal Minds: Beyond Borders* (from 2016; it was renewed for a second season).

CSI franchise, including *CSI: Crime Scene Investigation*, *CSI: Miami*, *CSI: NY* and *CSI: Cyber* (TV, various dates)

Somewhere, on some television network from Liverpool to Poughkeepsie, an episode of this multifarious *CSI* franchise is playing, supplying none-too-confrontational comfort television viewing that is rarely disturbing but always intriguing, even though the detectives are mostly unfeasibly handsome – few police departments in the real word boast killer cheekbones like those we see in *CSI*. And if that sounds like faint praise, it's possibly because the show's basic tropes are (inevitably) spread rather thinly over the wide variety of offshoots, with the individual attributes of the actors in each show carrying the weight of the drama. And because of this overextension, there is no denying that cliché has crept more firmly into this franchise than in most of its competitors. Nevertheless, when a viewer tunes into one of the show's tributaries – even halfway through – they will probably find themselves watching till the end.

THE DEPARTED (film, 2006)

Martin Scorsese's sure touch as a director of such crime classics as *Goodfellas* seemed to be in abeyance shortly before this resounding return to form. *The Departed* is a remake of the Hong Kong film *Infernal Affairs*, and has Scorsese's go-to actor Leonardo DiCaprio as a Boston cop going undercover to trap Mafia boss Jack Nicholson. Nicholson's career had been in something of a similar slump, but he found his customary eye-catching form under Scorsese's focused direction.

DEXTER (TV, 2006–13)

Jeff Lindsay's novels – in which a functioning psychopath working with the police kills other less winning psychopaths – was lucky enough to be made into this engaging but (without wishing to sound prissy) morally dubious series. Rather in the fashion that Coppola's *The Godfather* knowingly utilised the appeal of its leading players to allow us to ignore their murderous nature, we are always subtly on the side of the actor Michael C Hall against the variety of blood-spattered nasty opponents he is usually up against. It's a balancing act, as in the books, but – as Lindsay originally realised – a healthy dose of black humour makes the medicine slip down very nicely.

DRIVE (film, 2011)

To the real aficionado of American crime fiction, the name of the writer James Sallis conveys a pared-down, existential approach to the genre that might be described as quintessentially cinematic. Certainly his novel *Drive* proved to be a perfect springboard for Nicolas Winding Refn's nervy, forceful adaptation. The actor Ryan Gosling, on the cusp of the superstardom he is now enjoying, plays a character moonlighting as a getaway driver (there is a nod to Walter Hill's equally sparse and existential film classic *The Driver*) who aids a married neighbour (Carey Mulligan) on the run from gangsters. The extreme violence did not faze genre fans but accrued some mainstream criticism for the film.

END OF WATCH (film, 2012)

Written and directed by the talented David Ayer, *End of Watch* established a strong relationship between its stars Jake Gyllenhaal and Michael Peña as police colleagues and best friends; their spiky badinage is a particular pleasure of the film. The use of a hand-held camera at intervals grants an air of verisimilitude.

FARGO (TV, 2014–)

It's not always a risk converting a hit film into a television series, provided some surgery is performed on the original property; *McCloud* with Dennis Weaver, for instance, ripped off the central premise of Don Siegel's *Coogan's Bluff* but added its own individual touches. The Coen Brothers' wonderfully eccentric and (seemingly) haphazard original film – famous for its unglamorous (and pregnant) female cop played by Frances McDormand – was an influence on several subsequent shows. Perhaps sensing it might be an intractable property when it came to retooling for television, Noah Hawley created an anthology format for the show, and it proved to be a success – if, finally, it lacks the highly individual quirkiness of the original. English actor Martin Freeman was a canny addition to the series; the Coen Brothers, however, suggested that they were distinctly underwhelmed by the show.

GANGS OF NEW YORK (film, 2002)

In terms of conception, casting and creative talent, *Gangs of New York* had everything going for it, and admirers of Martin Scorsese were both surprised and disappointed that the film lacked the kind of highly individual vision that distinguishes his best work. Nevertheless, *Gangs* has much to offer in this tale of confrontation between criminal gangs in the Manhattan of the 1860s. Leonardo DiCaprio (notably under par) joins a gang to avenge the murder of his father, but his relationship with the gang leader played by Daniel Day-Lewis (in a self-consciously grandstanding performance) compromises his intentions. Visually, the film is stunning, and the sense of time and locale is perfectly evoked.

GONE BABY GONE (film, 2007)

While the actor Ben Affleck has recently donned the cape and cowl of the Dark Knight – and has a very respectable acting career – his most lasting achievement may be as a director. Like his predecessor Clint Eastwood, he has proved as adept at this discipline as he ever was as a thespian. There was a lot to lose in this adaptation of the ambitious novel by the author of *Mystic River*, Dennis Lehane, but Affleck drew together the strands of his intelligent film with great aplomb. Set in the working-class districts of Boston, the narrative involves the disappearance of a four-year-old girl. Private eye Patrick Kenzie (Casey Affleck) follows her trail with single-minded dedication – even as Affleck cannily consolidates our interest. There are superb supporting turns from Morgan Freeman and Ed Harris as cops on the same case.

GONE GIRL (film, 2014)

A film of Gillian Flynn's mega-hit novel was absolutely inevitable, but what was less predictable was that it would be both a critical and a commercial success. As in the previous entry – but here as actor rather than director (the film is directed by David Fincher) – Ben Affleck is as reliable as ever as the husband under suspicion after the disappearance of his wife (and the actor, commendably, does not attempt to ingratiate himself with the audience). But the real revelation here is the English actress Rosamund Pike in the title role, moving on from merely decorative roles to supply a performance of real complexity in what is essentially an impossible part. At a stroke, Pike considerably increased the esteem in which she was held.

HANNIBAL (TV, 2013–15)

While Thomas Harris has so far declined to furnish a satisfying resolution to his Hannibal Lecter saga (with his psychopathic anti-hero and vulnerable heroine Clarice Starling left in a bizarre sex slave situation), an entirely different challenge was presented to the makers of the television series that followed the various films – one that, in the event, they were not able to overcome. In as much as the series format (as opposed to a serial format) dictates that Hannibal has to remain in virtually the same situation at the beginning of each episode, there is never a sense of organic development among the characters or in the narrative – we're left with a Dexter-style scenario in which a murderous killer tracks other killers as bad as (or worse than) himself. End of episode – back to square one. In the title role, Mads Mikkelsen gleaned admirers, but didn't capture the ice-cold intellectual menace of the Anthony Hopkins or Brian Cox film assumptions of the role.

A HISTORY OF VIOLENCE (film, 2005)

While initially making his mark as a director of intelligent, provocative horror films, the Canadian filmmaker David Cronenberg has ventured (with considerable success) into the crime genre over the years, notably in the English-set *Eastern Promises* and this telling piece. Taking the basic premise of Hemingway's *The Killers* (and its subsequent film adaptations) – the ex-criminal who goes to ground and attempts to forge a new identity before being tracked down by his associates – Cronenberg grants the familiar scenario a more multifaceted and nuanced approach than we have previously seen in the various versions of this plot device, aided by a nicely ambiguous central performance from Viggo Mortensen.

IN PLAIN SIGHT (TV, 2008–12)

David Maples' crime drama stars Mary McCormack, Frederick Weller and Paul Ben-Victor. The show may frequently trade in the familiar – notably the fractious relationship between police colleagues – but finds some intriguing ways to subvert the clichés. And while the familial relationships in the show are cut from standard material, there is some attempt to make the variety of villains unlike those we have seen before.

INSOMNIA (film, 2002)

The history of Hollywood cinema is littered with ill-advised remakes of European films in which the very elements that made the originals successful are thoroughly leached out. And while the original Scandinavian film of this title (directed by Erik Skjoldbjærg) seemed ripe for such damage to be done, that proved not to be the case – hardly surprising, in fact, given the involvement of the director Christopher Nolan and the highly accomplished actors Al Pacino and Robin Williams. They may not bring the intensity to their parts of their Nordic predecessors, but their performances remain hypnotic.

JACK REACHER (film, 2012)

When this writer once gently suggested to Lee Child that the modest-sized Tom Cruise might not be the best choice to play Child's tall hero Jack Reacher, the author, smiling, replied, 'Do you think he's a good actor, Professor?' (That's what he calls me.) My answer was an unqualified 'yes'; he proved it in such films as *Rain Man*, in which he held his own capably against Dustin Hoffman. Much derision was directed at the casting of Cruise as Child's implacable, picaresque hero in Christopher McQuarrie's adaptation, but there is no denying that Cruise quietly nailed the part in a restrained but efficient film that steered clear of the improbable heroics of his *Mission Impossible* franchise. A sequel was to follow.

JUSTIFIED (TV, 2010–15)

While Elmore Leonard is possibly among the top three or four greatest modern American crime writers, filmed adaptations of his work have been hit or miss; ironically, the films of his Westerns *Hombre* and *3:10 to Yuma* are unqualified winners. This television series joined such successful film adaptations of Leonard as Barry Sonnenfeld's *Get Shorty* in capturing the author's highly individual approach to the crime fiction genre; the darkest humour is set against notably quirky, dialogue-heavy characterisation. What's more, in the five-year run of the series, more and more of Leonard's particular universe was successfully freighted into successive episodes. US Marshal Raylan Givens is dispatched from Miami to his childhood stamping ground of depressed rural coal-mining towns in Eastern Kentucky.

KAREN SISCO (TV, 2003–04)

Still with Leonard, this sharp series (all too brief in its run) has as its title character a female United States marshal – an Elmore Leonard creation – on Miami's Gold Coast. Deftly and efficiently made, this is worth seeking out.

THE KILLER INSIDE ME (film, 2010)

Any recommendations for British director Michael Winterbottom's visceral adaptation of Jim Thompson's novel have to come with a caveat: the film contains one of the most difficult to watch sequences in any crime movie, in which the psychopathic sheriff hero (chillingly played by Casey Affleck) systematically – and at some length – beats a woman to death. The sequence shares with a similar scene in Gaspar Noé's *Irreversible* the capacity to unsettle even the most violence-jaundiced of viewers. An earlier film version of Thompson's nihilistic novel had captured some of the pitch blackness at its centre, but Michael Winterbottom was the filmmaker who took audiences to the furthest reaches of a twisted criminal psyche.

KILLER JOE (film, 2011)

While various directors have either encouraged – or perhaps just not discouraged – the excellent actor Matthew McConaughey from using his barely articulated Texan accent in film after film with an attention to realism rather than comprehensibility (non-American audiences often struggle with the actor's naturalistic delivery of dialogue), there is no denying his sheer force and charisma. Everything he plays – including his efficient but largely unsympathetic character in this powerful piece – demonstrates his commendable refusal to play for easy likeability. The film is also something of a return to form for the director William Friedkin.

KISS KISS BANG BANG (film, 2005)

On its first appearance, Shane Black's comic thriller enjoyed some enthusiastic notices, if no great commercial success, and its reputation has grown over the years – suggesting that its strange mix of the comic and the violent was perhaps ahead of its time. It's interesting now to look at the performance of Robert Downey Jr; his reading of the dialogue seems like a prototype of what was to follow in his much-loved fast-talking characterisations in superhero movies.

LAW & ORDER (TV, 1990–2010)

Law & Order, the brainchild of Dick Wolf, synthesised both legal and police procedural elements and inaugurated a successful franchise. After its NBC run (beginning in 1990), it entered syndication, and the last season ran in May 2010. The show proved to be the most durable of crime series on US TV, with an impressive 20 seasons. The dramas were set in New York, often utilising real police cases, and a significant factor in the show's success was the fact that it achieved a strong homogeneity despite a large and disparate cast.

THE LINCOLN LAWYER (film, 2011)

Michael Connelly's second signature character (after Detective Harry Bosch) was given a very satisfactory cinematic incarnation in this slick adaptation, ably directed by Brad Furman, with the author's slippery low-rent – but essentially good-guy – lawyer Mickey Haller winningly played by Matthew McConaughey. Mickey's office is his chauffeured Crown Court Lincoln, and when he is engaged on the case of a rich man accused of trying to murder a prostitute, his complicated life becomes even more complicated. The plotting here is less important than the colourful characterisation, with such individual talents as William H Macy also shining in the cast.

LONGMIRE (TV, 2012–)

This solidly written series, created by Hunt Baldwin and John Coveny, is based on Craig Johnson's popular novels about the cool and efficient sheriff of Absaroka County in Wyoming. He is a character with painful inner conflicts who keeps such things ruthlessly at bay in professional situations. Commendable attention is paid to character development, notably in the title role by Robert Taylor (not the more famous actor of that name, of course).

MEMENTO (film, 2000)

The plot may now be familiar (not least from other crime narratives that have borrowed it), but Christopher Nolan's pre-Batman thriller is dispatched with both invention and originality, as Guy Pearce (excellent here, as he so often is) tries to deal with his lack of short-term memory. Unlike most current cinema, the audience is obliged to concentrate on what the film is saying – and it is all the better for it. It was clear from Nolan's debut feature that great things would follow.

THE MENTALIST (TV, 2008–15)

The central notion of Bruno Heller's show is novel: the principal character fakes psychic abilities to assist the California Bureau of Investigation (an organisation similar to the FBI), but is actually utilising his acute skill at psychological profiling to achieve results. Starring the *sotto voce* British actor Simon Baker in the title role, the show ran for seven seasons and reached a tally of over 150 episodes. With its charismatic star a key selling point, the show averaged 14 million viewers per episode over its entire run, and it was also nominated for the International TV Dagger at the Crime Thriller Awards in the UK. As so often in such shows, however, repetition was not always avoided.

MULHOLLAND DRIVE (film, 2001)

The reputation of David Lynch's phantasmagoric cult movie could not be higher, and most would agree that it is fully justified. This film's bizarre and surrealistic vision, almost a summa of the director's fractured world view, is a nightmare meditation on certain aspects of American society. The visuals have an almost feverish intensity as the relationship plays out between a film star, Laura Harring, suffering memory loss and an aspiring actress played by Naomi Watts. The film's ethos ranges from the erotic to the murderous and is brilliantly handled by both actresses (notably Watts, whose reputation was greatly burnished by this film).

MYSTIC RIVER (film, 2003)

Some crime films (notably *The Godfather*) improve upon the original material, while others traduce the novels on which they were based. Occasionally, however, an excellent novel is transformed into an equally excellent film – as was the case with Clint Eastwood's lengthy but intensely focused adaptation of Dennis Lehane's novel (from a screenplay by the talented Brian Helgeland). A group of childhood friends find their lives changed irrevocably when the daughter of one of their number is killed, obliging them to come to terms with this incident from their shared past. With the always-reliable Sean Penn, Tim Robbins and Kevin Bacon as the trio, Eastwood had a group of actors who could do full justice to his cogent vision.

NCIS (TV, 2003–)
This durable franchise actually began with *JAG* (1995–2005), utilising as protagonists military lawyers and standard police investigators. The show enjoyed a run of ten years, gleaning awards along the way. *NCIS* may be by some measure the number one television drama in the world – according to J Kingston Pierce – and it is definitely the most popular crime drama, having taken over from *Law & Order*. Offspring of the show include *NCIS: Los Angeles* (from 2009) and *NCIS: New Orleans* (2014 onwards). Its voracious appetite for story material has inevitably meant some recycling, but the changes are satisfyingly rung.

NO COUNTRY FOR OLD MEN (film, 2007)
Certain actors are born to play terrifying psychopaths (the diminutive Joe Pesci has made something of a speciality in this area), but one of the most implacable realisations of a terrifying murderer was delivered by Javier Bardem for the Coen Brothers in this remarkable thriller from Cormac McCarthy's novel. Vietnam vet Llewelyn Moss (played by Josh Brolin) discovers a drug deal gone awry and steals a suitcase containing millions of dollars. But soon on his tail is a merciless killer wielding a cattle prod – not to mention other drug dealers and a tenacious sheriff (Tommy Lee Jones). The film is both tough and decidedly bleak.

NUMB3RS (TV, 2005–10)
Produced by Ridley and Tony Scott, this solid crime drama features two brothers (like the Scotts?) who tackle crime in tandem; one is an FBI agent, the other a mathematician. With strong performances and a keen engagement with a variety of social issues, the show ran for six seasons and ratchetted up over 100 episodes.

NYPD BLUE (TV, 1993–2005)

Longevity is not always a guarantee of quality in television (look how long the woeful *Big Brother* franchise has lasted), but it is an indication of the achievement of this show which, like *Law & Order*, made its first appearance in the 1990s but continued into the new millennium. Created by Steven Bochco and David Milch, the show is now famous for the eternally growling, caustic copper played by Dennis Franz, channelling a variety of performances he had given in the films of Brian De Palma. Like many long-running shows, *NYPD Blue* visibly ran out of steam towards the end of its run, but Franz deservedly won praise for his portrayal of the character Andy Sipowicz. The show was also celebrated for the fact that real-life law enforcers praised *NYPD Blue* for its unglamorous authenticity.

OCEAN'S ELEVEN (film, 2001)

The Frank Sinatra/Lewis Milestone original may have been compromised by the laziness that affected so many of the actor's films (the exception being the John Frankenheimer classic *The Manchurian Candidate*), but the effortless cool of the Clan grants the film a retrospective sheen. So a certain chutzpah was required by George Clooney, Matt Damon and their associates to bring off this remake of the 1950s Las Vegas heist movie – and the younger actors' readiness to take it on proved highly successful, not least because of director Steven Soderbergh's nicely judged mix of fun and tension. Inevitably, sequels followed.

THE PLEDGE (film, 2001)

Friedrich Dürrenmatt's celebrated original novel is one of the classics of European crime fiction, with the story of a dogged detective's years-long wait to track down a killer incorporating a philosophical dimension not often seen in the genre. The actor Sean Penn (directing here) appears to juggle childishness and ego with the surest of filmmaking instincts when it comes to his output as both an actor and a director, and his work on this remarkable adaptation is a career best. He is immeasurably aided by Jack Nicholson, superb in one of his least mannered performances as the cop heavily weighed down by guilt.

RIPLEY'S GAME (film, 2002)

This writer once met Patricia Highsmith, who expressed to me – in no uncertain terms – her disappointment with Alfred Hitchcock's film of her first novel, *Strangers on a Train*; I politely demurred – but not too strongly, as she was a touch on the fearsome side and I was a very young journalist. In fact, Highsmith has been particularly lucky over the years with her film adaptations – and recently a rush of cinema versions of her books have been filling cinema screens. Her charming and murderous protagonist Tom Ripley has had a variety of incarnations (beginning with Alain Delon's take in René Clément's *Plein Soleil*, a version of *The Talented Mr Ripley*), and one would have thought that the versatile American actor John Malkovich – particularly adept at balancing charm and menace – would be perfect casting in this version of the novel *Ripley's Game*. But the director Liliana Cavani was clearly reluctant to rein in the stylised mannerisms that had often blighted Malkovitch's performances, and, equally damaging, her adagio pacing in the film keeps things just slightly below boiling point.

ROAD TO PERDITION (film, 2002)

Max Allan Collins' graphic novel has long enjoyed a following, and this film adaptation does it considerable justice, not least for the counterintuitive casting of Tom Hanks as an ice-cold hitman well aware of his parental responsibilities and an ageing Paul Newman as a deeply unpleasant mob boss. Sam Mendes, always a strong director of actors (as befits his stage directing experience), brings out the best in both of his performers. A pre-007 Daniel Craig is also on view, prior to being directed by Mendes in that role.

THE SHIELD (TV, 2002–08)

Taking the viewer into a sweaty inner-city Los Angeles police precinct, Shawn Ryan's gritty show may use the standard 'cops breaking the rules to get results' scenario but overfamiliarity is largely kept at bay with some inventive storylines, while the bullet-headed actor Michael Chiklis studiously avoids any bids for audience sympathy. Chiklis was subsequently to play an even more bullet-headed and violent character, *The Fantastic Four*'s Ben Grimm. The multi-stranded plotlines are refreshingly complex, although it has to be said that they frequently stretch viewer credibility. The edgy shooting style – while familiar from other shows – was influential on succeeding crime dramas.

SIN CITY (film, 2005)

Frank Miller has long been one of the most radical talents working in – and transforming – the comics medium with his design-led work. And while many would be happy with this level of achievement, Miller opted to make his mark in the cinema – and certainly did so with this visually breath-taking slice of neo-noir pulpishness, a heady goulash of detectives, violent criminals and femme fatales. The markedly stylised visuals (in which we can recognise, transformed in graphic novel style, Bruce Willis, Mickey Rourke and British actor Clive Owen) succeed in distracting us from the various plot elements that are essentially lovingly repurposed clichés of the genre; it might be argued that Miller was fully aware of the shop-worn materials he was tackling and of how his radical treatment would transform them. A sequel to the film made in 2014 was far less successful.

SONS OF ANARCHY (TV, 2008–14)

A project from the writers of *The Shield* (Kurt Sutter was a writer, producer and director on both shows), *Sons of Anarchy* proved to be as strong and accomplished as its well-thought-of predecessor. Avoiding the clichés of the police procedural, the show (uncompromisingly violent in nature) dealt with the members of a California biker gang, granting its unpromising premise genuine scope and ambition. *Sons of Anarchy* broke records for the FX cable network, surpassing the viewing figures of previous hit shows such as its predecessor *The Shield*. As well as gleaning strong audience approval, the show was also a critical success and was nominated for numerous Emmy Awards (which, controversially, it never won).

THE SOPRANOS (TV, 1999–2007)

Where to start with *The Sopranos*? In the twenty-first century, David Chase's groundbreaking show is universally recognised as one of the most important contributions to TV crime drama ever made, incorporating a richness and complexity rarely seen in the genre. And a particular achievement of the show is that most of its protagonists are a truly loathsome bunch of American Mafiosi; the balancing act performed here is making its murderous central character, Tony Soprano, not exactly sympathetic but allowing the viewer to become involved in his various problems, ranging from the elimination of criminal rivals to his panic attacks and his problems with troublesome offspring. Tacit audience collusion with the ruthless Tony is established in the teeth of any moral repugnancy we might feel, not least because of the late James Gandolfini's superbly rounded performance in the title role. There are those who feel that the ambiguous ending – we never learn the final fate of Tony – lacks the catharsis of the classical gangster tale.

THE TOWN (film, 2010)
Fiercely concentrated and brilliantly stage-managed, *The Town* is further evidence of Ben Affleck's considerable skill as a filmmaker. A group of bank robbers find that the bank manager they briefly took hostage may have the ability to identify them, despite the fact that they wore masks. Affleck's troubled central character is set against the underplayed FBI man of John Hamm. The film's study of loyalty and betrayal is highly persuasive.

TRAFFIC (film, 2000)
Steven Soderbergh has shown a marked affinity for the crime genre throughout his very varied career, and the faux-documentary style he adopts for *Traffic* pays dividends. With a variety of interlaced plot elements to deal with, the viewer is given a fascinating picture of the lines of supply for US drug culture. The large cast is uniformly excellent, but Benicio Del Toro in particular stands out as a compromised Mexican cop in one of the performances of his career.

TRUE DETECTIVE (TV, 2014–)
Nic Pizzolatto's remarkable crime show built up an almost unprecedented cult reputation that was very speedily torpedoed by the misconceived second series. In the first series, however – which looked and sounded like nothing else viewers had seen

before – troubled Louisiana State Police detectives Rust Cohle and Marty Hart find themselves being examined about a homicide investigation they previously worked on in 1995. Set against the interrogation scenes involving the two compromised principals, the solving of a ritual murder is proved to be not at all what it seems. So many elements of the show, notably its superbly realised visuals (including one kinetically shot chase around a suburban neighbourhood), gleaned praise – not least the mesmeric performances of Woody Harrelson and Matthew McConaughey (the latter constantly uttering gnomic and impenetrable philosophical remarks in an often incomprehensible accent). The show is in the upper echelons of televised crime drama; while the ending may have cheekily borrowed from a famous horror film (which I won't name here for the sake of *True Detective* virgins), it did not vitiate the effect of what had gone before. The fall from grace, however, happened with the second season of the show, with new actors and the virtual absence of all that had distinguished the inaugural series.

VERONICA MARS (TV, 2004–07)

The title character in Rob Thomas's enjoyable, sparky drama has worked in her teenage years as a private detective; she ends up back in her home town for a high school reunion and becomes involved in a criminal investigation. The striking performance by Kristen Bell is a notable plus factor here, and led to a movie that, rather than being an introduction to the series, assumed a total familiarity with the material on the part of the viewer. Certainly, for Bell's character alone, the series deserved a longer run than it received.

WINTER'S BONE (film, 2010)

The bush telegraph among reviewers of crime fiction and films is sometimes a useful guide to work that deserves attention, and that early warning system was quickly alive to the merits of this distinctive and atmospheric film directed by Debra Granik and adapted from the novel by cult writer Daniel Woodrell. The setting is a rundown shanty town in the Ozarks, and Jennifer Lawrence – an actress of prodigious skill – gives a career-best performance as a teenager obliged to arrange the life of her own disorganised mother and siblings when her father, a drug dealer, jumps bail and abandons them. The film is sharply observed, focusing on the ground-down life of its hapless protagonists, and has a trenchancy that makes it anything but a depressing experience. For once, an excellent crime novel has had salutary justice done to it in the film adaptation.

THE WIRE (TV, 2002–08)

A nigh-legendary crime drama. For five ever more ambitious and all-encompassing seasons, David Simon's sprawling Baltimore-set HBO crime series redefined the genre as fundamentally as *The Sopranos* had done previously, taking in drug culture, politics, business, unions and even the US teaching system. It was a series that aspired to being a modern vison of society to match that of Émile Zola. David Simon spent time with Baltimore's homicide police in 1988 and created a picture of the city – notably dystopian, despite his claims to the contrary – and its compromised police force every bit as idiomatic as his depiction of the drug dealers (both the kingpins and the grunts) who take up half the narrative. The show made stars of the British actors Idris Elba and Dominic West (both adopting totally persuasive American accents), while utilising such top-notch crime writers as George Pelecanos and Richard Price. The series has proved to be a tough act to follow, not least for showrunner David Simon himself.

WITHOUT A TRACE (TV, 2002–09)

Hank Steinberg's long-running show relies heavily on the solid presence of its leading players Anthony LaPaglia, Poppy Montgomery and Enrique Murciano to keep its slightly repetitive series of plotlines fresh. The show, for all its virtues, lacks the complexity of such crime dramas as *The Wire* (as discussed above) and tends to focus on emotionally driven storylines that can always be guaranteed to provide an instant frisson. What's more, the central characters are cast within a relatively limited developmental framework and display a prescribed set of characteristics each episode. The show does, however, incorporate an ironclad sense of pace and a careful attention to cinematography – the latter always utilitarian but impressive.

ZODIAC (film, 2007)

The director David Fincher is now acknowledged as one of the most ambitious and creative talents at work in Hollywood today, always demonstrating a commendable refusal to repeat himself. If *Zodiac* is firmly in the well-worn serial killer idiom, it nevertheless brings several unusual elements to bear in its tale of the real-life Zodiac Killer who terrified San Francisco in the late 1960s and 1970s, opening up a correspondence with the newspapers – just as his Victorian predecessor Jack the Ripper did with the police. The playing from a first-rate cast is exemplary, but Robert Downey Jr (as so often) steals the show with his larger-than-life reporter. Despite the measured, low-key approach taken by Fincher to his material, *Zodiac* remains quietly riveting.

4: Author Interviews

Although – in the final analysis – it is only the books that count, I've always found it useful to speak to as many of the crime writers from different countries as I can for insights into both their working methods and their philosophies. What follows is a selection of conversations I've had with key American crime authors.

JAMES ELLROY

'Fasten your seat belts – it's going to be a bumpy night.' Bette Davis's warning is something that any interviewer of James Ellroy might profitably bear in mind. His abrasive reputation is legendary, and the self-styled 'Demon Dog' of American crime fiction has also described himself as 'the greatest living crime writer', a *soi-disant* observation that a great many of his contemporaries – and thousands of readers – would agree with. False modesty is not James Ellroy's thing. But this man who has shaken out all the exhausted tropes of American crime fiction like loose nails, leaving behind something as ambitious, corrosive and unsettling as anything in the genre, is famously unsparing with interviewers: he has them for breakfast. This reputation was on my mind as I approached the Taj Hotel near Buckingham Palace (he was in the UK to promote his most recent novel, the gargantuan *Perfidia*). What's more, it had been communicated to me that he was none too pleased with my review of the book – even though I'd tried to suggest that the book's vaunting ambition made the work of most of his contemporaries seem like minnows in *Perfidia*'s formidable wake.

Certainly, no genteel, collegiate encounter was on the cards. This, after all, was a man who in his own abrasive autobiography *My Dark*

Places goes some way to explain why his work is often a descent into a neon-lit, hellish Los Angeles – and his own psyche. That book presented an unvarnished picture of his terrifying childhood. His mother was murdered when he was only ten years old, and his teenage years were a smorgasbord of drugs, alcohol and a variety of off-kilter sexual obsessions (which included raiding women's apartments for their underwear). A robust 66 at the time of the interview (2014), Ellroy has a reputation for taking no prisoners. Am I – in American argot – about to get handed my head?

There is little argument among aficionados that Ellroy's monumental L.A. Quartet (*The Black Dahlia*, 1987; *The Big Nowhere*, 1988; *L.A. Confidential*, 1990; and *White Jazz*, 1992) is the greatest of modern crime novel sequences. Starting with a relatively simple premise (a killing at an all-night diner is under investigation by three LA cops, each of whom has a very different agenda), Ellroy utilises the discursive narrative to produce a massive panoply of Los Angeles in the 1950s, more assiduously detailed than the work of that other great chronicler of the area, Raymond Chandler. Blending his fictional scenario with real events and characters, the picture-postcard vision of the city (with its non-stop sunshine, glistening beaches and universal prosperity) is swiftly undercut by Ellroy's penetrating view of the darker side, but his real subject is the psyches of his three very different police officers. It is in this area that the true greatness of the novels lies, for while the psychology of his protagonists is laid open with a scalpel-sharp precision, the task is always performed in prose that is as accomplished as anything in literary fiction. Perhaps the 'Great American Novel' might spring from the pen of marauding Visigoth Ellroy, writing about the defining era of post-World War Two America, stirring into his heady brew real-life figures such as JFK, cross-dressing FBI supremo J Edgar Hoover and gangsters such as Vito Genovese.

But then something happened: Ellroy's subsequent books were couched in an eccentric 'telegraphese', prose so spare (but dense) that it cost him many readers – while not, however, denting his reputation one iota. As I head towards the sumptuous Jaguar suite, I wonder: do I bring up this audacious change of method? My teeth are gritted.

But as James Ellroy walks into the room – tall, elegant, and with the look of a bookish intellectual rather than a volatile streetfighter – I suspect I'm in for a somewhat different experience from the one I expected. It seems my English politeness is a plus; Ellroy has a Hannibal Lecter-like respect for manners over all else, and tells me later that he has walked out of interviews in which he's felt that the interviewer has been rude.

So, where to start? A discussion of the massive *Perfidia*, perhaps? No; the first thing we discuss is how he feels about the news that the Republicans now rule the roost in the Senate and that Obama's presidency is of the lame duck variety. He hadn't heard the news, and is elated. 'Really? Is that the case?' he asks, grinning. 'That really pleases me – I can't wait to ring up my left-wing friends and rub that in.' So, I ask, is he an unapologetic right-winger?

'Well, I'm in the country of Margaret Thatcher and Winston Churchill, both heroes of mine – as was Ronald Reagan. In fact, all three shared something other than sensible right-wing views: a love of splendid, old-fashioned oratory.'

But oratory (in at least two of those cases) written by others, I demur...

'That doesn't matter!' smiles Ellroy. 'What they said – and how they said it – is what counted.'

To the book: I ask if Ellroy really needs to do this kind of promotional tour – exhausting, multi-country, multi-event. Surely his books will sell whether he publicises them or not?

'Yes,' he replies. 'But they will sell more if I do Manchester one night and Rome a week later. And I want to support my publisher. Besides' – he looks me in the eye – 'sometimes the boredom is allayed when I'm asked something I haven't been asked before.' No pressure for me, then.

How – in his sixties – are his energy levels for these kinds of junkets? 'I have terrific energy levels. And I'm good at husbanding my resources. I'm able to focus on the things that are important in my life and to cut out the crap. For instance, if a restaurant or bar is playing loud rock music – which I loathe – I simply get up and go. I cut short a meal the other night because the restaurant was simply too loud. If there is going to be music in my life, it will probably be Beethoven. Experiencing genius recharges one's own batteries and is immensely good for the soul. I don't allow myself too much untoward stimulation. I want fewer people in my life – I'm not looking for new friends. Most of the time I live in a sort of monkish seclusion; I see a friend and his wife, and we watch things like *The Killing* – both the American and the Danish versions. The original, incidentally, is about 30 times better. I don't assiduously read what my crime fiction contemporaries are writing, however.'

Ah, yes – the soul. Does Ellroy share with the Republicans whose victory pleased him a strong belief in God? 'Absolutely,' he answers. 'I'm able to find God everywhere, and that offers me the same solace as the music of Beethoven. After my grim childhood and a life that has hardly been peaceful, I know the value of things which now give me peace – such as God.'

But this isn't the iconoclastic figure I had been prepared for. I try to stir things up. Hasn't religion (I suggest) been the source of so much strife throughout history? The things done in the name of Christianity and Islam? But Ellroy is not to be provoked: 'We can hardly blame God for the things his followers do in His name, can we?'

'The murder of my mother is something that affected the subsequent course of my life – and continues to do so.' He smiles gently (something I'm realising is his default mode – no channelling of the 'Demon Dog' in this interview). 'My mother's killing… I always wonder how long it will take before it comes up in any interview.' (I avoid pointing out that it was Ellroy himself who brought it up.) 'Of course, that trauma was immensely influential for reasons I wrote about in *My Dark Places*, and the excessiveness of the event was perhaps a harbinger of the excessiveness of the life I was to lead – until now, that is.'

I also avoid mentioning that I'd written the review of *Perfidia* with which he was not best pleased, but ask him how he responds to the critical reception of any new book.

'*Perfidia* has had some… interesting reviews, some of which get the book wrong, but I don't review the reviews. I can't afford to take on board hostile criticism of, for instance, my attempts to take risks with language. But *Perfidia* is the first of a new quartet and then I'm thinking of writing a trilogy, and in all of these I'm planning to do something different.'

I ask if it's something of a Damoclean sword, being 'the greatest living crime writer'; that can't be too relaxing, can it?

'Fuck, no – it isn't, but writing is one area where I'm not looking to relax. I want to write better and better books. Sometimes the writing process is not an organic progression, but something shocking. *L.A. Confidential* – in its entirety – came to me as something of a synoptic flash, and in the backlash of that flash, I realised that whatever I could conceive, I could execute. It was a seismic, life-changing moment.'

Ellroy leans back and sips his mineral water; he doesn't drink any more. I am by now starting to wonder if the dyspeptic view of flawed humanity one gleans from his books is, in fact, illusory. 'I'm an optimist!' he exclaims. 'Whatever people may think, I have an ameliorative view of human nature. Sex, for instance, may be a deeply troubled area in my books – and many of my characters are deeply fucked up in that area. But I see sex as an expression of love and a very positive thing. Love and sex have always fuelled me.' But what angers him? 'Do you want to know what I really hate in people? Nihilism! That really pisses me off.'

Aha – so I've found an area that may channel a little of the Ellroy bile which has been conspicuously absent so far in our talk. One source of anger, surprisingly, is the youthful audience he spoke to in trendy Shoreditch in London the night before. 'Hipsters – God! They were all so nonconformist in an utterly conformist way; they all resemble each other; the fashion accoutrements are a straitjacket. I do find hipsters immensely self-regarding, and bizarrely enamoured of squalor in a rather effete way.'

But isn't Ellroy himself the hippest of writers? He smiles wryly.

'All I can say is that I like to surround myself with square people. I was never really "hip". The hipsters like rap: misogynistic, semi-literate doggerel. The voice of urban youth? Give me a break. Rap as art? Fuck, no! Art should encompass the world, open avenues and cross boundaries. At least it's what I try to do.'

SARA PARETSKY

Outside, the driving hail has Londoners hunching their shoulders against the elements, but in Victoria's well-appointed Goring Hotel, a comforting coal fire warms the equally well-appointed guests in the lounge. A few of these glance up as one of America's most celebrated crime writers walks in, but then their gazes flicker away; the celebrity of a crime writer – even one as prodigiously successful as Sara Paretsky – hardly matches that of glitzier trash celebrities. As ever, Paretsky quietly exudes the elegance and style that have become her hallmarks: she is slim and fit-looking, wearing her years very lightly indeed (a result, she says, of her rigorously maintained keep-fit regime). She is visiting a freezing London to call on old friends and to promote a provocative standalone novel, *Bleeding Kansas*, set in the county she grew up in before moving (like her female private eye VI Warshawski) to the more cosmopolitan Chicago. Paretsky takes a seat looking out on the garden walls of Buckingham Place; she is some distance away from more corpulent American hotel guests, and muses on the fact that obesity is not quite that simple class-led issue it might seem to be: 'In certain areas of Chicago, those involved in the service industries – mainly African Americans –- often tend to be heavily overweight, and that's probably due to bad diet as well as avoidance of exercise – no doubt that's true of working-class obesity in the UK.' She smiles. 'But the well-heeled Americans here have not piled on the pounds with burgers and fries – it will be expense account lunches and haute cuisine.'

Paretsky is also well known for her social commitment, and talks about serious issues in prestigious venues from New York to Oxford. After she orders a mint tea (she tells the waitress that the mint tea is the reason she stays at this hotel), Paretsky seems keen to talk about a hundred things rather than her work: the rise of religious fundamentalism in her own country; the Iraq war; the erosion of women's rights along with many of society's personal liberties. But her publicist has left her with a gentle admonition that it's necessary to mention *Bleeding Kansas* once or twice – and it's not a particularly difficult task, as the novel crackles with many of the issues that concern its author, sporting a narrative about religious intolerance in a conservative Kansas community thrown into disarray by a freethinking woman from the big city.

As she says this, Paretsky's penetrating blue eyes shine with intensity, but then her expression becomes opaque: wary and slightly guarded. Like her rival in the bestselling American crime fiction stakes, Patricia Cornwell, there is a certain vulnerability here: both women are aware of what a fragile-boned thing fame is, and Paretsky in particular always assumes the polar opposite of an Ozymandias-like 'Look on my Works, ye Mighty, and despair!' position – even though her sales and critical acclaim should give her good reason for a certain *amour propre*. But perhaps she is aware that the provocative, multi-stranded *Bleeding Kansas* is a harder sell than her effortlessly entertaining Warshawski books and may enjoy something of a mixed reception.

By now the lounge of the hotel is packed (with a card game at a nearby table), and the noise levels seem higher than one might expect from such an upscale clientele. As Paretsky gathers up the schedule given to her by her publicist, she wonders if she has been sufficiently coherent during the interview – self-deprecation is one of her most winning characteristics. As ever, of course, the answer is resoundingly in the affirmative. As anyone who has spent an hour in her company will tell you, you leave with an enhanced, open-eyed apprehension of the world we all live in, with both its injustices and its splendours.

She is quickly talking about one of her favourite themes: religion versus science. 'I see you have a great brouhaha at the moment about embryo research, with Catholic MPs and bishops lining up against those who want to advance medical science? I feel like I'm back in the US...,' she says sadly.

Has she seduced us with her diverting crime novels in order to sneakily slip us the big political book, where she grinds several axes?

'Not really! Frankly, one of the things I wanted to do in *Bleeding Kansas* was to try to explore what drives the Religious Right. I grew up in Kansas and I never imagined wanting to set a book back there, but there were several reasons why this particular book became something that I wanted to write. From the time that I first started thinking about it, it was a good ten years before I actually finished it, and I kept playing with it and not being able to move it forward. I sometimes think that maybe going back to the land of your childhood is... well, Thomas Wolfe said it... you can't go home again.'

Is the book – set in the state where she 'became the person

she is' (after an unhappy childhood with warring parents) – a way of exorcising personal demons?

'Well, it may have started that way, but such notions don't really work. I mean, I think if there were people you couldn't stand up to when they were alive, flogging their ghosts doesn't help you. I was hopeful I could do this, but it didn't work. On a physical level, however, I went way out of my way to burn down my childhood home.

'We were one of the few Jewish families in the area when I was growing up and the service man for the Sears Roebuck vacuum cleaners and so on that my mother used had belonged to a tiny sect that believed that Jews were the original chosen people of God so he would never charge my mother for a service call. And then on the other side, we had all the usual kinds of stereotypes about money-grabbing, etc. However, I didn't have any personal experience of anti-Semitism until I was in high school and I was asked to try to explain Judaism to religious groups who wanted to know why Jews controlled all the money in the world.

'We had a fundamentalist revival of religion in our high school – it was a small town with just one high school – and attendance was mandatory. It was really very frightening being taken in to the auditorium and the preacher would be bellowing at you for five hours on what your sins were, and during my final year in school the Supreme Court had just ruled that you could not have sectarian prayer in publicly funded schools and I and three Catholic girls whose parents didn't approve of that and one boy whose family were flagrant atheists went to the principal and demanded to be excused. And so we were taken and locked in this little room. I used to think about what would have happened if the school had burned down.'

Bad reviews – has she had any?

'You know, my favourite bad review – usually they just hurt my feelings – was for one of the VI books. *Time Out* here in London wrote that it was time for VI to retire to a home for deranged feminists and then I should follow her; my friends and I just said that this was such a wonderful idea – a retirement home for deranged feminists. So my husband suggested the name "Gelding Manor" – perhaps one of these sprawling Victorian mansions with turrets upon turrets.'

In fact, of course, Paretsky is very much a man-friendly feminist in person; her husband, a physicist who was an associate of Fermi, is much in her conversation. And her upbeat attitude concerning the relations between the sexes is part of an optimistic, if unsentimental, view of life.

'Grace Paley has this sentence in one of her short stories that I love: she says that "unlike life I am merciful to my characters". And life is too hard. When I read I don't want to be left utterly bereft. I just read Sarah Waters' *The Night Watch*, which I thought was a beautiful book, extraordinary in construction, but also a little bit too heartbreaking, and maybe I'm not a strong enough person to tolerate that much heartbreak.'

SCOTT TUROW

Speaking to Scott Turow in London a couple of years ago was a pleasurable experience. For the jaded crime fiction journo (who has perhaps spoken to too many none-too-stimulating American authors), it's deeply refreshing to encounter a writer whose engaging personal qualities are matched by a sharp intelligence. The conversation ranges over many issues, with his bestselling novels – such as his mega-selling *Presumed Innocent* – being only one among many topics, and it's hard to know what to spotlight first. How, for instance, does Turow regard his putative readers?

'I take my readers as I find them,' he says. 'There are those who are looking for a page-turning thriller; fine, I'm happy to provide that to the best of my abilities. Some want plausible details of how the courts and juries work; I'm pleased to have them on board too, as that's an area – in all modesty – that I know a great deal about.'

So why do we readers continue to have a fascination for the legal profession while regarding lawyers as something akin to pond life? (Though possibly higher up the evolutionary scale than bankers...)

'I think there is a plurality of values here,' replies the author. 'The law is the arbiter of values. And, of course, we're all cynical when there is a clear miscarriage of justice; for instance, when the OJ trial came to its famously controversial conclusion, many people felt a sense of outrage. But, on the other hand, if you're being prosecuted for a major crime, who are you going to call? A lawyer like Johnnie

Cochran, of course, who gets the job done. He used whatever material came to hand – he did his job, in fact, whatever we think of the result.'

Is Turow worried by the fact that so many legal thrillers are clogging up bookshops? A trend that he and John Grisham might be said to be responsible for?

'I don't think the market is in danger of being swamped yet. There appears to be a stable level of high interest, and for the time being, readers still seem fascinated by the legal thriller genre. But all these things are cyclical, aren't they? And, like all trends, this will pass, and only the best books will make an impact.'

Turow talks about his belief in science, and is briskly dismissive of the idea that America is rushing headlong towards a kind of dumbed-down religious state, despite appearances to the contrary.

'I think the Religious Right is in the minority, and they get more column inches than they actually deserve. They're on the back foot now, thankfully, although I imagine it doesn't appear that way to sceptical observers in the UK. Fortunately, many of us are more concerned with science, with the rational. I have a great faith in DNA, fingerprinting, ballistics – the latter is a key element in one of my books, *Reversible Errors*.'

Inevitably, we touch on the Hollywood success of the film of *Presumed Innocent* with Harrison Ford. 'All my books have been optioned, whether they get made or not,' says Turow. 'And that's both a good and a bad thing. After seeing the film of *Presumed Innocent*, I have to confess that – whether I liked it or not – Harrison Ford's face became mentally overlaid for me on the face of my protagonist. But in the end, it's the book that counts, isn't it? And that's the thing I'm responsible for.'

PATRICIA CORNWELL

There is absolutely no question as to who rules the roost in forensic crime fiction. After her first novel *Postmortem*, in 1990, Patricia Cornwell bagged almost every important crime award, and she consolidated her success with a sequence of books featuring the tenacious (if vulnerable) Dr Kay Scarpetta, now the definitive fictional forensic pathologist. Cornwell's books are a canny marriage of the traditional police procedural with something new: an investigation based on minutely detailed and gruesome posthumous evidence. Successive novels firmly fixed the author as a brand, and such books as *Blow Fly* made even the unsparing forensic detail of the earlier books look restrained, while Scarpetta's independence makes her deeply unpopular with her long-suffering bosses.

On a visit she made to London, I asked Cornwell some questions.

Can we talk about your roots?

'I was a crime journalist, but I didn't read crime fiction. I went on patrols at night with the police, investigating homicide scenes. My interest in pathology probably began when I heard about a death row inmate being beaten to death by fellow prisoners when I was on a 1980 night shift. I remember phoning up a nurse and asking about the victim's injuries. This question was met with some surprise, but basically I was taking the view of an archaeologist looking at a given set of circumstances. The morgue became a place of fascination for me.'

Why did you choose to have as your protagonist the forensic expert Kay Scarpetta?

'It was almost an accident that I began writing about crime. My ambitions, in fact, were to write a literary novel, but after I had had several books rejected by a publisher, I asked an editor what she felt was wrong. She replied: "You clearly want to write about your forensic pathologist character. Make her the centre of the book." After that, you might say, I didn't look back.'

Were you aware of creating – or at least changing – an existing genre, the forensic crime novel?

'Not at all. I didn't read my contemporaries – something that is to a large extent still true today – and I simply wrote what I had to. *Postmortem* was not an immediate success, though it had something of a *succès de scandale*: it was banned in Richmond – people would say that they were disturbed by the fact that a woman was at the centre of all this violent activity. But basically I didn't have a clue about what else was being written in the genre, and I really had no intention of shaking it up.'

It goes without saying that you seem to relate to Scarpetta, your pathologist protagonist, more than to any of the other characters.

'Undoubtedly. As a journalist, I was always keenly interested in the basic facts; very much the approach for Kay Scarpetta. I do share one other thing with Kay: a respect for the real life behind the bodies. But, as for identifying with her, I try to place myself in the minds of all my characters.'

You obviously have extensive experience of real-life forensic situations.

'Yes, enough for many books. But the science is changing all the time and I try to keep up with that.'

How do you feel about the criticism directed against women such as yourself who write violent crime fiction?

'Ironically, I always get that question in Britain more than in the US. My first response is that women are the principal victims of crime, so why shouldn't we write about it? Actually, in the US, it's not the violence as much as other aspects of the books that are likely to upset the Religious Right, such as the fact that my character Lucy is a lesbian.'

There are so many people now who write in the Patricia Cornwell style – do you try to keep up with them or any of your other peers?

'Actually, I make a point of not reading crime writers as I am wary of being influenced by something I've read. At the moment, for instance, I'm reading a biography of the writer William Golding.'

KATHY REICHS

Why does she do it? Why does Kathy Reichs – so comfortably at the top of the tree in the crime-writing stakes – put herself through the punishing publicity grind for each new book? Surely, at this stage of her career, she can afford to put her feet up and let the inevitable healthy sales follow? It's a question I put to her in her bijou London hotel on a gloomy Monday morning.

She sighs – and smiles. 'Actually, to be frank, I still quite enjoy the whole publicity process – whenever I'm in a given city talking about my books, I'm fine – it's fun. It's just getting there; it's the travelling which is such a drudge. If there were some way I could circumvent that boring bit of the process, then everything would be absolutely perfect.'

Kathy Reichs has a full CV; she is vice president of the American

Academy of Forensic Scientists, a member of the RCMP National Police Services Advisory Council, forensic anthropologist for the province of Quebec and a professor of anthropology at the University of North Carolina-Charlotte. She is also a frequent expert witness in criminal trials. In 2001 she was called in to join the National Disaster Recovery team after the Twin Towers terror attack on New York. She worked around the clock for two weeks – sifting through the rubble for traces of human remains and packing it up for medical analysis. She has also testified at the United Nations tribunal on the Rwandan genocide and helped to identify people buried in mass graves in Guatemala.

Her first book, *Déjà Dead*, quickly became a *New York Times* bestseller and won the 1997 Arthur Ellis Award for best first novel. All of her Temperance Brennan novels have been *Sunday Times* bestsellers. Reichs – no underachiever – is also a consultant on the TV series *Bones*, which features her character Brennan, and is the author of a forensic series aimed at young adults, including the titles *Virals* and *Seizure*.

Since I last spoke to her, she remains as busy as ever – and is clearly showing absolutely no signs of slowing down. But does she plan to take things easier at some point?

'I'm more than happy keeping busy – ultra-busy – with all my various activities,' she replies, 'including the forensic consultancy work. And I have one thing that keeps the latter stimulating for me – I can, in fact, pick and choose the cases that I want to work on. If I feel a particular case is not for me, I can refer it onwards. So I'm always working on a case that has a particular interest or fascination for me.'

Given that expert witnesses have been getting a particularly hard time in Britain lately, discredited for the wrong decisions, has she noticed that syndrome in the States – the credentials of expert witnesses being questioned, for instance?

'Those credentials *should* be questioned,' she replies firmly. 'It has to be said that there are some people out there who are claiming to be forensic experts who are no such thing. They have just done some very basic training at the fringes. Their parameters are very narrow – and such people are prone to comment on areas that they really don't know enough about. The thing for any witness to do in such a scenario is to simply say "I don't know" – in other words, don't expose yourself if you're out of your comfort zone where your knowledge is concerned.'

Déjà Dead established Reichs' reputation in 1997, and Temperance Brennan made an immediate mark as a solid and reliable heroine. By the time of *Death du Jour*, Reichs had begun to consolidate and refine elements present in the early books and clearly established her as a truly impressive writer, decisively moving her out of the shadow of Patricia Cornwell. With *Deadly Decisions*, the consolidation process continued – including through frequent festival invitations. I ask her how her appearance at the 2012 Cheltenham Literature Festival went (we had both done panels there but our paths had not crossed).

'Oh, I really enjoyed it,' she replies. 'Despite the rain (and even the hail, which I managed to miss). I had a very lively panel with Val McDermid.'

The mention of McDermid prompts a mention of a familiar issue – one that now bores the Scottish Crime Queen: did the usual 'violence and female crime writers' question come up?

'It usually does, but I think I'm in pretty safe territory,' Reichs replies. 'Actually, I never use gratuitous gore in my work. I tell the reader the truth – unsparingly – about what happens to the human body, but to some degree I think that is my duty as a writer, isn't it?'

5: The Thirty Best Contemporary US Crime Novels

Before you ask 'Where's James Ellroy?', remember that the criterion here is work written in the twenty-first century – and while Perfidia *(2014) has its considerable virtues, it's hardly the equal of* L.A. Confidential, *published in 1990. And Thomas Harris's* Hannibal Rising *(2006) is some distance in achievement from 1988's* Silence of the Lambs...*

The titles below are in no particular order, and I had wry discussions with both J Kingston Pierce and Craig Sisterson about the foolhardy task of compiling such a list.

Dennis Lehane – *Shutter Island*
Sara Paretsky – *Critical Mass*
Tom Franklin – *Crooked Letter, Crooked Letter*
Robert Crais – *Suspect*
Attica Locke – *Black Water Rising*
Daniel Woodrell – *Winter's Bone*
Greg Iles – *Natchez Burning*
Michael Connelly – *The Lincoln Lawyer*
James Lee Burke – *Jolie Blon's Bounce*
Gillian Flynn – *Gone Girl*
Bill Beverly – *Dodgers*
Thomas H Cook – *Sandrine's Case*
Harlan Coben – *Gone for Good*
John Hart – *Down River*
Megan Abbott – *Die a Little*
James Sallis – *Drive*
Peter Swanson – *The Girl with a Clock for a Heart*

American Noir

Derek B Miller – *Norwegian by Night*
Don Winslow – *The Power of the Dog*
James Carlos Blake – *The Rules of Wolfe*
Laura Lippman – *I'd Know You Anywhere*
Walter Mosley – *Little Scarlet*
George Pelecanos – *Right as Rain*
Martin Cruz Smith – *Wolves Eat Dogs*
Dan Fesperman – *The Double Game*
Richard Price – *The Whites*
David Morrell (Canadian, but US-adopted) – *Murder as a Fine Art*
Wiley Cash – *A Land More Kind Than Home*
Michael Farris Smith – *Desperation Road*

And an entry by a non-crime writer:
Michael Chabon – *The Yiddish Policemen's Union*

6: The Five Best Contemporary US TV Crime Shows

Breaking Bad (2008–13)
Boardwalk Empire (2010–14)
The Sopranos (1999–2007)
True Detective (2014–)
The Wire (2002–08)

Acknowledgements

I'm indebted to J Kingston Pierce of *The Rap Sheet*, Craig Sisterson, Ayo Onatade and Kim Newman, along with my fellow newspaper crime critics Jake Kerridge, Marcel Berlins, Laura Wilson and John Dugdale, for both stimulating discussion and hard facts. I'm always ready to stand corrected – as we nominal 'experts' should always be.